PSALMS/
PROVERBS

PSALMS/ PROVERBS

JACK W. HAYFORD
Executive Editor

THOMAS NELSON
Since 1798

NASHVILLE   DALLAS   MEXICO CITY   RIO DE JANEIRO   BEIJING

Published in Nashville, Tennessee. Thomas Nelson is a trademark of Thomas Nelson, Inc.

Thomas Nelson, Inc. titles may be purchased in bulk for educational, business, fundraising, or sales promotional use. For information, please email SpecialMarkets@ThomasNelson.com.

Hayford, Jack W.

Psalms/Proverbs

ISBN 13: 978-1-4185-3329-8

Printed in the United States of America
1 2 3 4 5 6 7 8 9 10 — 16 15 14 13 12 10 09 08

TABLE OF CONTENTS

PREFACE

Pursue Wisdom...

WHY WOULD GOD so fervently tell His people to pursue wisdom? Wisdom is holistic insight into the true nature of things. It is a God-given ability to discern right and wrong, cause and effect. It is the ability to separate fact and fiction, truth and deceit. It is the ability to most effectively apply knowledge. It begins with the fear (profound respect and submission) of God and finds its solution and conclusion in Him.

Wisdom is not some profound ability conferred on the aged, nor is it something that intellectual knowledge alone can bring, though that is a part of wisdom. Only our heavenly Father can illuminate wisdom within our spirits, hearts and minds. Only through Him can we learn to properly appropriate or apply knowledge.

Our desire should be to gain wisdom through each encounter with life. Whether trial or success, joy or sorrow, wisdom awaits us.

As you delve into this in-depth look at wisdom, allow the Lord to speak to your heart. Allow Him to bring vibrant life into the knowledge of Him and His kingdom. The way of wisdom is the way of truth, virtue and peace. The way of wisdom is the way to God's Way.

"Wisdom is the principal thing; therefore get wisdom. And in all your getting, get understanding. Exalt her and she will promote you; she will bring you honor, when you embrace her. She will place on your head an ornament of grace; a crown of glory she will deliver to you" (Proverbs 4:7–9). Remember, when we ask for wisdom, we receive God every step of the way. May you be enriched and enlighten as you grow deeply in God's wisdom.

Keys of the Kingdom

K EYS CAN BE SYMBOLS of possession, of the right and ability to acquire, clarify, open or ignite. Keys can be concepts that unleash mind-boggling possibilities. Keys clear the way to a possibility otherwise obstructed!

Jesus spoke of keys: "And I will give you the keys of the kingdom of heaven, and whatever you bind on earth will be bound in heaven, and whatever you loose on earth will be loosed in heaven" (Matthew 16:19).

While Jesus did not define the "keys" he has given, it is clear that He did confer specific tools upon His church which grant us access to a realm of spiritual "partnership" with Him. The "keys" are concepts or biblical themes, traceable throughout Scripture, which are verifiably dynamic when applied with solid faith under the lordship of Jesus Christ. The "partnership" is the essential feature of this enabling grace; allowing believers to receive Christ's promise of "kingdom keys," and to be assured of the Holy Spirit's readiness to actuate their power in the life of the believer.

Faithful students of the Word of God, and some of today's most respected Christian leaders, have noted some of the primary themes which undergird this spiritual partnership. A concise presentation of many of these primary themes can be found in Kingdom Dynamics feature of the *New Spirit-Filled Life Bible*. The *New Spirit-Filled Life Study Guide Series*, an outgrowth of this Kingdom Dynamics feature, provides a treasury of more in-depth insights on these central truths. This study series offers challenges and insights designed to enable you to more readily understand and appropriate certain dynamic "Kingdom Keys."

Each study guide has twelve to fourteen lessons, and a number of helpful features have been developed to assist you in your study, each marked by a symbol and heading for easy identification.

 Kingdom Key

KINGDOM KEY identifies the foundational Scripture passage for each study session and highlights a basic concept or principle presented in the text along with cross-referenced passages.

Kingdom Life

The KINGDOM LIFE feature is designed to give practical under-standing and insight. This feature will assist you in comprehending the truths contained in Scripture and applying them to your day-to-day needs, hurts, relationships, concerns, or circumstances.

Word Wealth

The WORD WEALTH feature provides important definitions of key terms.

Behind the Scenes

BEHIND THE SCENES supplies information about cultural beliefs and practices, doctrinal disputes, and various types of background information that will illuminate Bible passages and teachings.

Kingdom Extra

The optional KINGDOM EXTRA feature will guide you to Bible dictionaries, Bible encyclopedias, and other resources that will enable you to gain further insight into a given topic.

Probing the Depths

Finally, PROBING THE DEPTHS will present any controversial issues raised by particular lessons and cite Bible passages and other sources which will assist you in arriving at your own conclusions.

The New Spirit-Filled Life Study Guide is a comprehensive resource presenting study and life-application questions and exercises with spaces provided in the study guide to record your answers. These study guides are designed to provide all you need to gain a good, basic understanding of the covered theme and apply biblical counsel to your life. You will need only a heart and mind open to the Holy Spirit, a prayerful attitude, a pencil and a Bible to complete the studies and apply the truths they contain. However, you may want to have a notebook handy if you plan to expand your study to include the optional KINGDOM EXTRA feature.

The Bible study method used in this series employs four basic steps:

1. *Observation.* What does the text say?
2. *Interpretation.* What is the original meaning of the text?
3. *Correlation.* What light can be shed on this text by other Scripture passages?
4. *Application.* How should my life change in response to the Holy Spirit's teaching of this text?

The New King James Version is the translation used wherever Scripture portions are cited in the *New Spirit-Filled Life Kingdom Dynamics Study Guide* series. Using this translation with this series will make your study easier, but it is certainly not imperative and you will profit through use of any translation you choose.

Through Bible study, you will grow in your essential understanding of the Lord, His kingdom and your place in it; but you need more. Jesus was sent to teach us "all things" (John 14:26; cf. 1 Corinthians 2:13). Rely on the Holy Spirit to guide your study and your application of the Bible's truths. Bathe your study time in prayer as you use this series to learn of Him and His plan for your life. Ask the Spirit of God to illuminate the text, enlighten your mind, humble your will, and comfort your heart. And as you explore the Word of God and find the keys to unlock its riches, may the Holy Spirit fill every fiber of your being with the joy and power God longs to give all His children. Read diligently on. Stay open and submissive to Him. Learn to live your life as the Creator intended. You will not be disappointed. He who promises you is faithful!

ADDITIONAL OBSERVATIONS

INTRODUCTION

Psalms and Proverbs

PSALMS AND PROVERBS are both part of the division of the Bible known as Wisdom Literature. (Wisdom Literature also includes Job, Song of Solomon and Ecclesiastes.) These books provide us with a better understanding of some of the most practical and down-to-earth truths about life. Both of these books are written in a poetic style, communicating emotion and allowing us to experience the feelings of the characters and hear within their words the very heart of God.

Wisdom Literature focuses on daily human experience in the world God made. Wisdom is an attribute of God, part of His divinity, given by Him to us so that we might live abundant, satisfying lives (Proverbs 2:6). When you read wisdom in the Bible, you don't usually find stories about God's judgment on sinful humanity in the last days, the coming of the Messiah, or God's actions in history to save His people. Instead, you find guidance for everyday life.

Psalms

The Hebrew title of the book of Psalms is *Sepher Tehillim,* which means "Book of Praises." The individual psalms may have been written during the years which extend from the Exodus to the restoration of Israel after the Babylonian exile. The book reflects the worship, devotional life, and religious sentiment of approximately one thousand years of Israel's history.

The imagery, style, and parallelisms (an archaic form of poetry depending on sentence structure rather than rhyme or meter) of some of the psalms reflect a very ancient Canaanite style and vocabulary. These beautiful, poetic discourses are actually a compilation of several ancient collections of songs and poems written by many different authors, some known and some unknown, including David (who wrote 75 of the Psalms), Moses, and Solomon.

There are a number of overriding themes in the Psalms: wisdom, creation, joy, sorrow, trust, fear, protection, thanksgiving, God's word, the Messiah, repentance, salvation and witness. For our purposes in this study, we will be focusing on the "wisdom" Psalms: 1, 14, 15, 37, 47, 50, 90, 94, 112, 127, and 128. These are the Psalms whose major message is the contrast between the "wicked" and the "righteous." Different sources group these Psalms differently, but all agree that great wisdom is found in the beautifully poetic book of Psalms.

Proverbs

The Book of Proverbs groups several collections of wise sayings which God inspired and directed to be kept in written form. From these proverbs we can learn how to deal with life, even before some situations occur. The way of wisdom is to learn and live, not live and learn. God has provided all the help we need to live a righteous, abundant life—His Spirit, His Word, and His people (2 Peter 1:3, 4). As part of His written Word, Proverbs aims at wisdom for daily living. The ultimate result of following God's ways is the experience, even now, of everlasting life.

Jesus loved proverbs and used many such sayings to teach His disciples. When His hometown friends refused to believe in Him, He responded with a proverb: "A prophet is not without honor except in his own country and in his own house" (Matthew 13:57). He explained to His disciples that people misunderstood John the Baptist's ministry as well as His own, again with a proverb: "Wisdom is justified by her children" (Matthew 11:19). On yet another occasion, when He taught about His second coming, Jesus used a proverb which was probably as well-known to the people then as "Where there's smoke, there's fire" is to us today. Jesus used this earthy proverb to underscore the sad fall of Jerusalem near the time of the final judgment: "For wherever the carcass is, there the eagles will be gathered together" (Matthew 24:28).

The word *proverb* comes to English from a Latin word that means "a word, speech, or discourse." The Hebrew word is *mashal*, which includes the core idea of "comparison." Indeed, we shall see that most proverbs compare a positive action with a negative one, such as

"The hand of the diligent shall rule,
But the slothful man shall be a slave" (Proverbs 12:24).

Understood broadly, the biblical proverb also includes riddles and word puzzles. Biblical and Eastern literature frequently use the proverb as a literary technique to make their writings enjoyable and memorable.

Word Wealth—*Proverb*

Proverb: Hebrew *mashal* (mah-shahl); Strong's #4912: a Proverb, parable, maxim, adage; a simile or allegory; an object lesson or illustration. This noun comes from the verb *mashal,* "to compare; to be similar." Based on the Book of Proverbs, it might appear that a proverb is a short saying containing a nugget of truth. Yet, Old Testament evidence shows it has broader uses. It can be a long discourse (as that of Balaam in Numbers 23—24), it may be a taunt, a byword, or an illustration. It may even be a person or a nation out of which God has made an example.

The Beginning of Wisdom

Wisdom is the intelligent use of knowledge that gives insight. It enables discernment and accurate understanding that leads to righteous choices. Proverbs seek to impart such wisdom to people of all ages; giving youth a standard by which all decisions can be weighed, and adding to the wisdom of the mature so they may live well, as well as guide others to follow God's ways. Life poses many curious, hard-to-understand problems. Proverbs will enlighten us and give us discernment about these puzzles as Psalms will lead us to proper and godly response. God does not want us to live in the dark, to be victims of vanity and foolishness. He longs for us to grasp wisdom and embrace praise—the two together will lead us into lives of abundant joy and promise.

How do we begin to become wise? The beginning of Proverbs tells us: We come to God. We respect and reverence Him in all submission and humility. "The fear of the Lord is the beginning of knowledge, but fools despise wisdom and instruction" (Proverbs 1:7). To "fear" the Lord means to acknowledge His great power, His complete authority over us and all creation, and His hatred of sin that can lead to judgment. But, it also means that we are to acknowledge His tremendous love and mercy toward us, and His goodness. Life has no meaning without God. He is the point, the reason, for all existence. We come first to Him for help, for guidance, for training, so that we may live abundant lives, serving God in good works, and leading others to His grace and salvation.

Read Psalms 145:3–20; 2 Timothy 3:16–17; John 10:10; 14:11–14, 15:1–10; Acts 1:8.

Questions:

What are signs that one possesses wisdom?

_____

_____

_____

_____

In what way will wisdom affect your relationships with God and others?

_____

_____

_____

_____

What actions and attitudes will wisdom always engender?

_____

_____

_____

_____

Preparation

In order to prepare adequately for understanding and realizing the course of wisdom to be found in the books of Psalms and Proverbs, read through the 31 chapters of Proverbs and at least the eleven Psalms upon which we will be focusing in the coming weeks: Psalms 1, 14, 15, 37, 47, 50, 90, 94, 112, 127, and 128.

Questions:

What relationship do you immediately find between the Psalms and Proverbs?

_____

_____

_____

_____

_____

_____

How are praise and wisdom related?

_____

_____

_____

_____

_____

ADDITIONAL OBSERVATIONS

SESSION ONE

The Way of Blessing
Psalm 1

 Kingdom Key—*Avoid Evil*

Proverbs 4:14–15 Do not enter the path of the wicked, and do not walk in the way of evil. Avoid it, do not travel on it; turn away from it and pass on.

To be confident in your own ability to avoid contamination by close contact with evil is foolish. Trusting in your own spiritual strength in the presence of temptation is dangerous. Even heroes of the faith such as Moses and David fell under the weight of temptation. How then can we consider ourselves immune to the lure and power of sin?

Proverbs offers the wise counsel to avoid evil; to steer totally clear for yourself and refuse to even walk alongside those who choose to toy with sin. Satan will tempt whenever, wherever and as often as he possibly can. He actually banks on our inability to withstand temptation. Wisdom demands that we do whatever it takes to turn our backs on anything that tempts us to sin.

Read Psalm 1:1–3; Proverbs 8:32–36; 2 Timothy 2:22.

Questions:

What are the temptations in your own life?

_____

_____

_____

_____

_____

What are some practical steps you can take to begin to experience victory over them?

✎ _____

_____

_____

_____

Experience Blessing

Psalm 1:1 begins with the word "Blessed." It is the first word in the book of Psalms and in it lies the essence of what is promised to those who read and meditate on all the psalms.

To experience the blessings prepared for us by God, we must remain constantly aware of the influences in our lives and the power they can hold sway over our spiritual destiny. In the remainder of Psalm 1:1 we discover a progression of acceptance: walks, stands, sits. This progression strongly suggests the profound effect outward influences can have on the forward momentum of our spiritual walk. What begins as a mere passing observance gains our attention and soon we "take up residence" with the ungodly.

Read James 4:6–8; Proverbs 1:15–16; 4:18–27; 10:23–25.

Questions:

What are those things of the world that gain your attention to the detriment of your spiritual walk?

✎ _____

_____

_____

_____

What blessings do you forfeit by entertaining this temptation?

✎ _____

_____

_____

_____

How can you actively resist this temptation?

_____

_____

_____

_____

What are the "issues of life?"

_____

_____

_____

_____

Word Wealth—*Blessing/Blessed*

Blessing: Hebrew *beᵉrâkâh* (ber-aw-kaw'); Strong's #1293: has at its root the word *bârak* (baw-rak') which means to kneel in adoration. At its very core *beʳrakah* speaks humility; the recognition of one's dependence upon the source of blessing. A blessing is a conveyed desire, whether spoken or demonstrated in act, for prosperity, success, and well-being.

Blessed: Hebrew *'ashar* (ah'-shar); Strong's #833: Happy, blessed, prosperous, successful, straight, right, contented. Its original meaning is "be straight." In Genesis 30:13 Leah gave birth to a son and said, "I am happy, for the daughters will call me blessed." She named this son "Asher" (from 'ashar), meaning "Happy One." Both the Messiah and the nation of Israel will be called "blessed" ('ashar) by the whole world: "Men shall be blessed in Him; all nations shall call Him blessed" (Psalm 72:17); "And all nations will call you blessed, for you will be a delightful land" (Malachi 3:12).

Kingdom Life—*A Blessed Life*

God helps us live the abundant life. Many people seek shortcuts to success; they often take advantage of others and bring all kinds of trouble upon themselves. But the only way to live a truly good life, one with health, integrity, and respect, is to speak and do what is right, according to God's definition. You may not receive the acceptance of the world, but you will receive the blessing of God.

Read Proverbs 10:22; 11:11, 26; 24:25.

Kingdom Extra

The idea of blessing can be understood in one of four ways. First, the patriarchs and leaders of Israel blessed their sons and younger generations to bestow on them certain privileges, responsibilities, and wealth (Genesis 27).

Also, blessings are good things given by God which bring happiness (Deuteronomy 28:8). A third concept of blessing is the "invocation of God's favor upon a person" (Genesis 27:12). Finally, a gift is also a blessing (Joshua 15:19).

Look up the following passages and tell the meaning of "blessing" in each one.

Read Psalms 1:3; 15:9–15; Luke 24:53; Galatians 3:14; James 3:10; Revelation 5:12, 13.

Questions:

What is similar among these occurrences of "blessing"?

_____

_____

_____

In what ways do these occurrences express different nuances of meaning for "blessing"?

_____

_____

_____

_____

How do you experience "blessing" in your own life?

_____

_____

_____

_____

Word Wealth—*Meditates*

Meditates: Hebrew *hagah* (hah-gah); Strong's #1897: To reflect; to moan, to mutter, to ponder; to make a quiet sound such as sighing; to meditate or contemplate something as one repeats the words. *Hagah* represents something quite unlike the English "meditation," which may be a mental exercise only. In Hebrew thought, to meditate upon the Scriptures is to quietly repeat them in a soft, droning sound, while utterly abandoning outside distractions. From this tradition comes a specialized type of Jewish prayer called "davening," that is, reciting texts, praying intense prayers, or getting lost in communion with God while bowing or rocking back and forth. Evidently, this dynamic form of meditation-prayer is very ancient and was practiced in David's time.

Contemplation of Excellence

Given the definition of "meditates" found in the Word Wealth article above, it would seem nearly impossible to remain in constant contemplation of God's truth. Throughout the centuries many have attempted to discover ways to achieve this state of mental and spiritual unity. Special religious orders have been formed whose stated and sole purpose was to pursue a life of meditation and communion with the Lord.

However, this first Psalm also states that the one who meditates "shall bring forth fruit" and "whatever he does shall prosper." These phrases don't seem to equate to a life removed from the business of life. They speak of a productive and thriving way of life—a way of abundant blessing and prosperity.

If the child of God can "pray without ceasing" (1 Thessalonians 5:17) and "thank God without ceasing" (1 Thessalonians 2:13), then it is also possible to "meditate day and night" (Proverbs 1:2) on God's truth. Psalm 1 exhorts us to strive toward a constant state of communion and fellowship with God; it must then be within our ability to achieve.

Read Psalms 4:4b; 19; Philippians 4:8; Isaiah 26:3.

Questions:

What is the result when one meditates on God's blessing and truth?

_____

_____

_____

What would be the effect of this meditation on: depression, worry, anger, fear?

✎_____

_____

_____

_____

The Flesh Is Weak

In the 26th chapter of Matthew we read of the agony Jesus experienced in the Garden of Gethsemane. His cruel death was at hand and He struggled within Himself.He was "exceedingly sorrowful." The Greek word used here is *perilupos*, (per-il-oo'-pos) meaning a profound, complete, excessive grief; a heaviness of soul that is beyond sorrow. To suffer *perilupos* is to experience an all pervasive emotional crisis of bewilderment, fear, uncertainty and anxiety. There is no other place in Scripture where grief is portrayed in such vivid terms.

Jesus struggled fiercely, not from fear of death, but from dread of being out of communion with His Father. He would become sin in order to defeat the power of sin. In so doing, would be left without the fellowship of God, for God cannot have communion with sin. In order to win victory over sin and offer us the New Covenant in His blood, Jesus had to willingly allow His relationship with God to be severed at the very time when He needed His Father the most. The dread of losing that relationship, even temporarily, caused Jesus to struggle to the point of sweating blood.

During this profound inner struggle, Jesus relied on His three most treasured friends for support and prayer. Yet they failed Him miserably. He requested only that they stay near Him and pray, but they slept. During Jesus' most traumatic inner struggle, His friends deserted Him, first in effect and then in deed.

His words to them reveal to us the battle we continue to fight: "Watch and pray, lest you enter into temptation. The spirit indeed is willing, but the flesh is weak." "Temptation" refers to a trial that entices one to be untrue to God. Behind such enticements are often demonic forces (see Mark 1:12–13), who will not hesitate to use weaknesses and limitations to lure the unsuspecting into wrong spiritual choices.

In this is found the reason that we are charged to meditate day and night, to pray without ceasing. Only in this can we be assured that we will be able to stand when the day of trial comes.

Read John 5:19; Ephesians 6:13–18; Proverbs 3:1–4; 8:34–36; 20:13.

Questions:

What can you learn about blessing from Jesus' struggle in the garden?

_____

_____

_____

If we act, as Jesus did, only according to what we "see" God doing, what effect will this have on our ability to resist temptation?

_____

_____

_____

How will the determination to act only as we are lead by God cause us to abide in His presence?

_____

_____

_____

_____

What other Scriptures can you discover that speak of the importance of meditating on the truths of God?

_____

_____

_____

_____

Record Your Thoughts

Reread Psalm 1.

Questions:

In your own words, describe the relationship between blessing and the avoidance of evil.

✎ _____

_____

_____

_____

Do you often meditate on the Word of God? If not, what hinders you and why?

✎ _____

_____

_____

If so, what has been the result in your life and relationships?

✎ _____

_____

_____

_____

What particular temptation remains a constant struggle for you?

✎ _____

_____

_____

How might you find victory over this temptation?

✎ _____

_____

_____

_____

The Way of Righteousness

Psalm 14

 Kingdom Key—*Know the Lord*

Proverbs 3:5–6 Trust in the Lord with all your heart, and lean not on your own understanding; in all your ways acknowledge Him, and He shall direct your paths.

Two words in this Proverb are especially significant—the words "ways" and "acknowledge."

The word "ways" (Hebrew *derek*) means: a road, a course, or a mode of action. It suggests specific opportunities a person may encounter on a recurring basis. This passage tells us that the Lord will direct our path, our journey, when we acknowledge Him with every opportunity: with each new day, with each new circumstance, with each new breath.

Of even greater significance is the word "acknowledge" (Hebrew *yada'*). In other passages *yada'* is translated as "know," meaning to know by observation, investigation, reflection, or firsthand experience. But the highest level of *yada'* is found in direct, intimate contact, as the life-giving intimacy in marriage. In a spiritual context, it implies an intimacy with God that conceives and births real life. We might conclude that maintaining *yada'*, or direct, intimate contact with God, brings the assurance of God's promise to show us the way to true, vibrant, and vital life in, with, and through Him.

Read Psalm 37:5–6; Philippians 3:7–11.

Questions:

What would be the result in a life fully committed (put in the hands of; given over to) the Lord?

_____

_____

_____

_____

Does your relationship with the Lord take precedence in your life?

_____

_____

_____

_____

What things do you struggle to give over to the Lord?

_____

_____

_____

_____

How does holding on to these things negatively affect your spiritual life?

_____

_____

_____

_____

How will knowing God increase your ability to trust Him?

_____

_____

_____

_____

Word Wealth—*Direct*

Direct: Hebrew *yashar* (yah-shar); Strong's #3474: To be straight, right, upright, pleasing or good. *Yashar* appears in an intensive form here and means to make straight and right. God will straighten out the path of His devoted, trusting servants. From this verb comes the noun *yosher,* meaning uprightness (Psalm 119:7). Job is described as blameless and upright (Job 1:1). God promised to make the crooked places straight (Isaiah 45:2). Finally, from *yashar* comes the poetical name Jeshurun (Upright One), a name always applied to Israel as God's righteous nation.

Kingdom Life—*Trust unto Righteousness*

Once we have set our course to truly know God, to become intimately acquainted with Him, our ability to trust Him will increase dramatically. As we discover who He is and begin to recognize His ever-present faithfulness and love, we can respond with nothing less than absolute trust.

However, trust in God is a choice. Too many Christians exercise weak or sporadic trust in God because they are lacking in their knowledge of Him and are therefore unprepared to commit to trusting Him. Trust as it is used in our Kingdom Key Proverb (*bâtach*) means to be totally reliant and unsuspecting. It is a complete, unquestioning, established, and unshakable confidence. This trust is convinced of the absolute fidelity and reliability of the One in whom trust is placed. This trust is possible only in a heart that seeks to know God and chooses to believe His word.

We have learned that those who will commit their way (lives) and place their trust in God will be led by Him. Those who are led by God will be led toward righteousness. To be righteous is to be in right-standing before God. This right-standing is accomplished through the shed blood of our Lord; through His death on our behalf. When we believe in and receive new life from our Lord, we become "the righteousness of God in Him" (2 Corinthians 5:21).

Those who trust in the Lord enjoy security and can rest assured in the priceless rewards from the Lord. They receive the reward of His love and protection. They receive the satisfaction of knowing the Lord smiles on their confidence in Him. But the greatest reward received by those who place their trust in God is the surety of their ascent to righteousness in Him.

Read Psalm 5:11–12; Habakkuk 2:4; Romans 1:16–17; Hebrews 10:35–38; 1 Timothy 6:11; 1 John 2:29; 3:4–10; Word Wealth below.

Questions:

What is the relationship between trust in God and faith?

_____

_____

_____

_____

In what way are righteousness and choice related?

_____

_____

_____

_____

What effect does being in right-standing before God have on your actions and attitudes?

_____

_____

_____

_____

How would righteous choices affect your relationships with others? With God?

_____

_____

_____

_____

Word Wealth—*Righteous*

Righteous: Hebrew *tsaddiq* (tsahd-deek); Strong's #6662: One who is right, just, clear and/or clean; a person who is characterized by fairness, integrity, and justice in his dealings. *Tsadaq* (the root of *tsaddiq*) and its derivatives convey a lifestyle of justice and integrity. Being righteous brings a person light and gladness (Psalm 97:11). This word is used to describe God Himself and occurs 66 times in Proverbs alone. According to Habakkuk 2:4, it is the *tsaddiq* who shall live by faith.

Behind the Scenes—*Revealing Words*

Throughout Proverbs the importance of words is highlighted. The Bible reveals to us that spoken words are not just empty vibrations floating through the air. They have power and meaning. They go forth to accomplish things (Isaiah 9:8; 45:23; 55:11; Proverbs 12:6). They possess a strange and wonderful power, which many modern people do not realize. They cannot be "taken back" or replaced. Once spoken, words affect other people, and they reveal the heart and soul of the person who speaks them (Matthew 12:34; 15:11, 18; James 3:8–12).

While our spoken words reveal much to the world, the words that we hide inside, the thoughts and ponderings of our hearts, can set the tone of our days and determine the course of our lives. In Proverbs 12 we read that intentions and thoughts will lead to condemnation or deliverance; as we think in our hearts, so we will be (Proverbs 23:7). Character and conduct begin in the mind. Our actions are affected by the things we dwell on in our thoughts. It is for this reason that Scripture exhorts us to concentrate on things that will result in right living (righteousness) and in God's peace (Philippians 4:13).

Read Proverbs 10; Psalm 19.

Questions:

When do you find it most difficult to "guard your tongue?"

How have "the words of your mouth" affected your relationships in the past?

✎_____

_____

_____

_____

If others could hear the thoughts of your heart, what kind of person would they find you to be?

✎_____

_____

_____

_____

How could what you have learned in this section improve your life?

✎_____

_____

_____

_____

A Proper Relationship

Proverbs 1:7 tells us that the "fear of the Lord is the beginning of wisdom." The greatest reward that comes from wisdom is the knowledge of God. Wisdom, then, is vitally connected with knowing God and having a proper relationship with Him.

Scripture tells us God will bless us exceedingly if we seek wisdom. The Lord Jesus told us something similar in Matthew 6:33: seeking the rule of God over our lives and His righteousness (His ways to do rightly), will open the way for God to bless our lives. Rather than being preoccupied with the pursuits of this world, our ambition should be to seek God and His righteousness, knowing that He has pledged Himself with covenant faithfulness to respond by providing all we need, in this life and in the world to come. God will reward those who are led forward by the voice of wisdom and diligently seek Him.

That righteousness brings reward is not a mechanical guarantee of cause and effect. Rather, like sowing and reaping, it is a general law built into the nature of God's world. It is an inexorable law of the universe; an absolute reality.

Read Psalm 14:2; Hebrews 11:6; Proverbs 3:7–8, 3:13–26.

Questions:

What do you believe is meant by "fear of the Lord?"

_____

_____

_____

_____

How can this begin the process of attaining wisdom?

_____

_____

_____

_____

In what ways have you experienced God's law of rewarded righteousness?

_____

_____

_____

_____

Kingdom Life—*A Disciplined Life*

Righteous living demands self-discipline (also known as self-control which is a fruit of the Holy Spirit). Where that discipline is lacking, God will provide correction. Often this correction of our thoughts, attitudes or actions will be supplied through difficult circumstance. Too often, we blame the devil, or the church, or anything or anyone else when trials or difficulties come our way. It may be that God is using these problems (which we have most likely created for ourselves because we have strayed from His ways) to teach us and correct us.

Christians are called by God to live righteous, holy lives of responsible, wise behavior. Foolishness, poor choices and ungodly behavior not only destroy our witness to the world but will also destroy our lives. By trusting God with all the situations of life and responding positively to His correction, we will be greatly blessed and be able to bless others as well.

Read Proverbs 3:11–12; Genesis 40:1–23; Numbers 22:15–34; Ruth 1:1–22; Daniel 1:1–21.

Questions:

In each of these passages of Scripture, God used a life situation to train and instruct. What can we learn from each?

_____

_____

_____

_____

What past difficult situation in your own life did God use for instruction and correction? What did you learn?

_____

_____

_____

_____

How can placing blame for difficulty hinder God's work in our lives? How can it hinder our relationship with God? With others?

_____

_____

_____

_____

Live in Righteousness

Clearly, God is interested in righteousness. He is holy and hates sin. He wants to protect us and provide for us in this life as well as the life to come.

Read Psalm 14:5; 1 Corinthians 10:13; 2 Peter 1:3, 4; Exodus 19:5; Colossians 1:9–14; Romans 5:1–5.

Questions:

What has God done to help us live righteous lives?

_____

_____

_____

_____

How should this affect the way you live and relate to others?

_____

_____

_____

_____

Record Your Thoughts

Reread Psalm 14.

Questions:

In your own words, describe the relationship between righteousness and knowing God.

_____

_____

_____

_____

_____

_____

What is your immediate reaction when difficulties overtake you and even linger or increase?

_____

_____

_____

_____

What does this say about your view of God?

_____

_____

_____

_____

What do your words tell others about you, your faith and your God?

_____

_____

_____

_____

During your free time, what types of thoughts most often occupy your mind?

_____

_____

_____

_____

The Way of Character
Psalm 15

Kingdom Key–*Give Generously*

Proverbs 11:25 The generous soul will be made rich, and he who waters will also be watered himself.

The character of a Christian should reveal devotion to the interests of others; the thoughtfulness of rendering untiring care; the delight in the prosperity, honor and happiness of someone besides oneself. The Christian life should reflect the heart of our Lord who gave all that He is so that we could know life. He gave that we might live, we give that we may know abundant life.

Read Matthew 20:25–28.

Questions:

Would others describe you as a giving person?

_____

_____

_____

_____

What does that reflect about your understanding of generosity?

_____

_____

_____

_____

What do you believe God is saying to your about your willingness to give?

✎_____

_____

_____

_____

In Giving We Receive

There is a universal law (principle) of divine reciprocity. You give; God gives in return. When you plant a seed, the ground yields a harvest. That is a reciprocal relationship. The ground can only give to you as you give to the ground. You put money in the bank and the bank returns interest. That is reciprocity.

Jesus opened up a whole new way of giving. We can no longer pay or sacrifice our way into God's mercy. Jesus Christ has paid our debt before God, and His Cross is a completed work in our eternal interest. Our giving, then, is no longer a debt that we owe, but a seed that we sow. The life and power source are from Him. We simply need to act on the potential that exists in the "seed-life" He has placed in us by His power and grace.

Abundance begins with investment. If you do not sow, you do not reap. If you do not give of yourself: your commitment, and resources, how can you expect to receive?

Read Luke 6:38; Matthew 25:14–29; Proverbs 3:33; 19:17.

Questions:

Why do you think it is so important to God that we learn to be givers?

✎_____

_____

_____

_____

_____

What seeds have you sown that have increased the lives of others?

_____

_____

_____

What effect has this giving had on your own life?

_____

_____

_____

What is the most difficult thing for you to give?

_____

_____

_____

Why do you think this is so?

_____

_____

_____

The Giving of Resources

God associates Himself with the poor by taking their plight personally. He promises to repay those who care about the marginalized and show kindness to the poor. Sheltering a homeless family, befriending a frightened stranger, visiting a despondent prisoner, or feeding a hungry child is a wise investment. The Lord Himself will repay us—not necessarily with wealth and comfort, but with the honor of reflecting His character by the sacrifice we make on behalf of the poor. Read Proverbs 19:17; Psalm 41:1–3; Mark 12:41–44.

Questions:

Locate other New Testament passages that speak of giving.

✎_____

_____

_____

_____

What is the effect in the inner man when giving becomes a lifestyle?

✎_____

_____

_____

_____

What must exist within before one can become a truly sacrificial giver?

✎_____

_____

_____

_____

The Giving of Commitment

The greatest commandment is to love and serve the Lord. This requires a continuous, conscious commitment of all that we have and are. We are told repeatedly in the New Testament that if we love God, we must also love others; if we serve Him, we must serve others as well.

The law of reciprocity is at the heart of all relationships. "Whatever you want men to do to you, do also to them" (Matthew 7:12). How profound an effect this "golden rule" would have if applied at every level in our world!

You would not want a neighbor to steal your tools, so do not take his. You would not like to be struck by a reckless driver, so do not drive recklessly. You would want a helping hand in time of need, so help others in need. In industry, we would not want the person upstream from us polluting the river, so we should not do it to the person downstream from us. We would not want to breathe chemically polluted air, so we should not pollute someone else's air. In the workplace, we would not want to be oppressed, so we should not oppress our employees. If applied, this kingdom law would remove the need for armies, jails, and prisons; social problems would be relieved, the burden of government reduced and the productive energies of all the people released. "Do unto others as you would have them do unto you," if put into practice, would revolutionize our society. This is the kingdom foundation for all social relationships.

Read Psalm 15:1–3; Matthew 25:34–45; Proverbs 11; 14:21, 31; Psalm 37:5–6.

Questions:

How does the "law of reciprocity" govern the words you speak?

_____

_____

_____

_____

Take an honest look at the problem relationships in your life. What have you sown into these relationships?

_____

_____

_____

_____

What does integrity demand of you and what specific steps can you take to improve your relationships?

_____

_____

_____

_____

Word Wealth—*Commit*

Commit: Hebrew *galal* (gah-lahl); Strong's #1556: To roll, roll down, roll away, remove. In Genesis 29:3, *galal* refers to rolling the stone from the well's mouth. In Joshua 5:9, the reproach of Egypt is rolled off from Israel. The message of this word is to roll all issues of life into God's care. The picture is of a camel, burdened with a heavy load; when the load is to be removed, the camel kneels down, tilts far to one side, and the load rolls off.

Kingdom Life—*The Reward of Giving*

God actually invites people to verify His trustworthiness with their giving. He promises that those who give will be placed in position to receive great, overflowing blessings. You can experience the windows of heaven actually opening with blessings you will not be able to "receive" or contain! He will cause every blessing that has your name written on it to be directed to you, and satan himself cannot stop it. Don't be afraid to try and see if God will bless your giving of time, resources and love; He is God and He will stand the test every time.

Read Malachi 3:10.

Question:

This verse refers to the giving of tithes. In what way might it also refer to giving of other resources?

✎ _____

_____

_____

_____

Kingdom Extra

Read Job 1:1–11.

We live in a world of "you scratch my back and I'll scratch yours." For many, this principle of give-and-take-extends to their faith. Ask them why they believe in

God and they'll reply that it's because of all the wonderful things He has done for them. In effect, their walk with God operates on the basis of reciprocity: He gives to them, and in exchange they follow Him.

Satan accused God of having that kind of relationship with Job. He charged Him with "buying" Job's loyalty by rewarding Job with wealth and security. As satan accurately pointed out, purchased devotion is suspect because it is liable to vanish the moment the rewards cease.

However, satan misjudged Job's character. Stripped of his possessions and struck with the tragic loss of his family, Job nevertheless blessed the name of the Lord and refused to blame God for his troubles. Later, when satan touched Job's body, he still refused to turn away from God asking if one should accept only good from God, and not adversity.

Job's integrity was a powerful response to satan's question, "Does Job fear God for nothing?" The answer was *yes*, Job feared God for nothing in return. His devotion was not bought; it was a gift.

Could the same be said of you? Do you follow God because of the "rewards" you believe He has given you? Suppose they were all taken away. Would you still honor Him? Is your commitment to the Lord out of a simple, genuine faith—the kind of steadfast faith that declares, "Though He slay me, yet will I trust Him" (Job 13:15)?

Record Your Thoughts

Reread Psalm 15.

Questions:

Explain the relationship between godly character and a generous spirit.

In what ways do you see the "law of reciprocity" being enacted in your life?

✐_____

_____

_____

_____

What changes can you make in your way of life that will positively affect this?

✐_____

_____

_____

_____

What do you find most difficult to give? Why do you believe that to be the case?

✐_____

_____

_____

_____

SESSION FOUR

The Way of Abundance

Psalm 37

Kingdom Key—*Persevere*

Proverbs 13:4 The soul of a lazy man desires, and has nothing; but the soul of the diligent shall be made rich.

Jesus said, "Ask, and keep on asking; seek and keep on seeking; and knock and keep on knocking" (Matthew 7:7: paraphrased). The Greek present tense emphasizes continuous action: Jesus was not saying knock once and stop, but keep on knocking until the door is opened. God, in His wonderful wisdom, has built the world in such a fashion that only those who are diligent and who persevere win the highest prizes. The person who is determined to achieve his God-given goal, despite all obstacles, will wind up a winner. Those who are fainthearted and faltering, whose minds are not made up about something, will always lose.

God makes us reach high for the better things. Only a few will strive hard enough to win them. Those who keep going in spite of problems, pain, and difficulty will eventually overcome them.

It is necessary to be persistent for God's blessings to truly flow in and through your life. The apostle Paul proudly declared, "I have fought the good fight, I have finished the race, I have kept the faith" (2 Timothy 4:7). In whatever task God places you, do not quit, but stay the course.

Read Psalm 37:34; Proverbs 3:27–28; 12:24, 27; 13:4; 13:21; 15:19; Galatians 6:7–10; John 10:10.

Questions:

What instances in Scripture do you recall where persistence resulted in reward?

_____

_____

_____

_____

In what ways do godly determination and persistence appear in your own life?

_____

_____

_____

_____

Describe your understanding of "abundant life."

_____

_____

_____

_____

Word Wealth—*Abundance*

Abundance: Hebrew *perisseuo* (per-is-syoo-o); Strong's #4052: To superabound in quantity or quality, overflowing, more than enough, extraordinary amounts, to have excess or surplus, above the ordinary, more than sufficient.

Kingdom Life—*Abundance Is God's Plan*

God's covenant to us is a covenant for abundant life. From the very beginning of time, Scripture shows us that God wanted us to be happy and prosperous. In Genesis, we are told that God made everything and declared it to be good. Then

He gave this beautiful, plentiful Earth to Adam; Adam was given dominion over all the Earth. God's plan from the beginning was for man to be enriched and to have a prosperous and abundant life. Christ came to Earth in defense of life. He revealed to us that it is God's intention to recover and restore to man what sin has stolen. By His words and actions He opposed any thing, force, or person that might diminish the lives of His people. Through the atoning death of our Lord, we are released from the power of sin and its consequence. God has reinstated, through Christ's defeat of our enemy, our ability to attain the abundance that He created and still desires for His people. By His death and resurrection, Christ has opened a new dimension of life for all mankind.

Likewise, He calls us to do everything within our power to preserve and enhance the lives of those around us. In addition to evangelizing, we are to work to reduce poverty, disease, hunger, injustice, and ignorance.

Read Psalm 37:3–9; Proverbs 21:5; 2 Corinthians 5:17; Matthew 6:25–33; Luke 12:15–34.

Questions:

What things in life hold the most power to cause you to worry or experience fear?

_____

_____

_____

_____

_____

In what ways do you experience lack in your life?

_____

_____

_____

_____

_____

What do you believe hinders you from experiencing the abundant life promised by our Lord?

✎ _____

_____

_____

_____

_____

Kingdom Extra—*Prosperity Revealed*

While it is clear that God wants His children to prosper, we must never lose sight of the fact that financial plenty is only one face of prosperity. This type of prosperity is of least importance in the kingdom. We have God's promise that He will always supply all that we need in the material realm: food, clothing, etc. He is our provider and will see to our needs. About those things, the child of God need have no concern.

Prosperity should never be equated to a place of ease and contentment and should never be an end in itself. It ought to be the result of a quality of life, commitment, dedication, and action that is in line with God's Word. Divine prosperity is not a momentary, passing phenomenon, but rather it is an ongoing, progressive state of well-being. It is intended for every area of our lives: spiritual, physical and emotional, even more so than material.

Read Psalm 37:4–11; Matthew 5:5; 3 John verse 2.

Questions:

What do you believe "inherit the earth" means?

✎ _____

_____

_____

_____

_____

How can your soul prosper?

✎ _____

_____

_____

_____

In what ways do you experience the Lord's prosperity in your life?

✎ _____

_____

_____

_____

Word Wealth—*Prosper*

Prosper: Greek, *euodoo* (yoo-ad-o´-o); Strong's #2137: to succeed in reaching, a successful journey as in achievement of a way of thinking or course of conduct. *Euodoo* also implies help received along the road or along one's way.

Patience Along the Way

We learned in the previous session that the law of reciprocity is much like sowing a seed. And God has a timetable for every seed we plant, everything we sow into the kingdom. His timetable is not always our timetable. Sometimes He provides a quick return for our labor, but sometimes the harvest can take years—even a lifetime. No matter the time required, we can count on the fact that God *will* cause a harvest to come from our seeds. His timing is rarely our timing, but we can rest assured that God is never early or late—He is always right on time with our best interests at heart.

Abundant life is, without doubt, God's will for us. But that abundance will take many forms and sometimes look nothing like what we expect. Our abundant harvest will have the same nature as the seeds sown: good seeds bring good harvests, bad seeds bring bad harvests.

What are we to do during the growing time of our seeds, while we wait for the harvest? (1) Refuse to become discouraged. (2) Determine to keep our faith alive and active. (3) Give and keep on giving; love and keep on loving. Know this—His harvest is guaranteed. Continue in an attitude of expectancy. Abundance will come, prosperity will arrive as we travel and allow the Lord to order our steps.

Read Psalms 37:3–11; 40:1–3; Galatians 6:7–9; Isaiah 40:31.

Questions:

What is the relationship between trusting the Lord and patience?

_____

_____

_____

_____

_____

How does discouragement affect your spiritual life?

_____

_____

_____

_____

_____

What is the effect on your relationships when discouragement over-takes you?

_____

_____

_____

_____

_____

Kingdom Life—*Giving As to the Lord*

Whenever we give, or plant our seeds of faith, we are doing it for Jesus. The person we feed becomes as Jesus to us. The person we visit in prison or in the sickbed becomes as Jesus to us. How may we know our Lord? We know Him in doing His works and in doing them as much to Him as for Him. We know Him in putting our arms around those who are desperate or alone. He said that when we do this we are putting our arms around Him—Jesus Christ, our blessed Savior.

Although our giving is to take on very real and tangible forms as we reach out to people, as we give through individuals and churches and ministries to meet great needs around the world, the focus of our faith is to be on Jesus and Jesus alone. He is God He is our Source. He is the object of our worship and our love. He alone is worthy of our lives, and He alone can supply our needs.

We give to others, but let us keep our vision clear. We look past them, with our faith directed to God and offered as a service of love for Him.

Our Savior Himself tells us what we can expect when we follow His principles for planting: a multiplied harvest! An abundant return is harvested when seed is sown wisely. When you give something to God, He will give it back in a way that is even better. How great is our God! We have no lack in Him—only potential!

Read Proverbs 1:24–26; 13:7; 3:9–10; Mark 4:1–20; 2 Corinthians 9:6–11.

Questions:

What seeds have you sown into the kingdom for which you have reaped a harvest?

_____

_____

_____

_____

What are some of the ways the Lord has multiplied your giving?

_____

_____

_____

_____

How will focusing on service to the Lord affect your willingness to give sacrificially?

✎_____

_____

_____

_____

_____

What are some areas where giving is a struggle for you? What do you think causes this struggle?

✎_____

_____

_____

_____

_____

Record Your Thoughts

Reread Psalm 37.

Question:

How do you understand the relationship between perseverance and abundance?

✎_____

_____

_____

_____

_____

We receive abundantly from the Lord so that we can give freely. It is a cycle of blessing in which we can be participants. Diligence in pursuing the things of God, diligence in prayer, diligence in service:

these are the things that produce an abundant harvest of righteousness, peace and joy and a life filled with all the goodness of God.

Questions:

In what ways are you an active participant in this cycle of blessing?

_____

_____

_____

_____

_____

_____

What would be the difference in your relationships if you remained constantly aware of God's call to diligence in pursuing holiness, in prayer and in service?

_____

_____

_____

_____

_____

We are to walk as Jesus walked. How will this fact impact your desire and ability to give?

_____

_____

_____

_____

_____

_____

ADDITIONAL OBSERVATIONS

SESSION FIVE

The Way of Humility
Psalm 47

 Kingdom Key—Recognize God's Preeminence

Proverbs 15:25 The Lord will destroy the house of the proud, but He will establish the boundary of the widow.

Pride will tell us we are self-sufficient. It will cause us to trust in our own ability and our own defective wisdom. Pride will lead us down the path toward selfish living, because pride esteems self above all else.

However, true knowledge of God leads to humility. Humility is not the self-deprecation with which many of us are often acquainted. Rather, it is the refusal to trust oneself for fulfillment of needs, looking instead to the Lord.

Understand that trusting in your own abilities is a vain hope. Exalting yourself will lead only to a painful fall into reality. You cannot find righteousness or the way to please God within yourself. Know that only Christ's imputed righteousness can allow us to stand before God. Diligently avoid any form of pride which leads to self-righteousness. Understand that pride will make you unteachable and unshapable in God's hand. Humble yourself regularly in the presence of the Lord. Let Him be the One to lift you up.

Read Psalm 47:8–9; Proverbs 15:33; 16:9; 16:18; James 4:6–10.

Questions:

In what ways do you fall into the trap of self-sufficiency?

In what ways is an independent attitude prideful?

_____

_____

_____

_____

How does pride interfere with God's plan for your life?

_____

_____

_____

_____

How does pride interfere with your relationships?

_____

_____

_____

_____

Word Wealth—*Humility*

Humility: Greek *tapeinophrosune* (tap-eye-nof-ros-oo-nay); Strong's #5012: Modesty, lowliness, humble-mindedness, a sense of moral insignificance, and a humble attitude of unselfish concern for the welfare of others. It is a total absence of arrogance, conceit and haughtiness. The word is a combination of the Greek *tapeinos* meaning humble, and *phren* meaning mind. The word was unknown in classical, non-biblical Greek. Only by abstaining from self-aggrandizement can members of the Christian community maintain unity and harmony among themselves and with God.

Kingdom Life—*Know in Your Heart*

Whenever we come to the Lord, the condition of our heart is of utmost importance. We must have a heart that acknowledges *who* God is and *what* He is like (Hebrews 11:6). We must also have a heart that recognizes God's abilities to meet our needs. It is this understanding of His greatness contrasted with our own insufficiency that humbles us before His throne.

Coming to God with humility is an absolute imperative. Still, too many have confusing ideas of what humility really is. We live in a world that thinks of humility as some order of a "see yourself as a worm" proposition. This is in no wise the case. True humility has everything to do with a person of power in the Kingdom of God and nothing to do with being ashamed of who God has made you to be. When our sinful shame is forgiven through Christ, God's view of us is as *treasured ones*. Examine how these verses describe God's view of you as His own: Malachi 3:17, 18; Ephesians 2:4–6; 1 Peter 2:9, 10.

Humility is living your life according to these truths—the truth about your righteous estate in Christ. The truth about God's mightiness and His tender grace and the truth about yourself and others and our great need demonstrates God's great grace.

Read Psalm 47:2; Proverbs 11:2; 15:13; Psalm 24; Proverbs 29:23.

Questions:

How can humility lead to powerful Kingdom living?

_____

_____

_____

_____

_____

How can pride lead to idolatry?

_____

_____

_____

_____

_____

What are some areas of pride in your life?

_____

_____

_____

_____

How have they affected your walk with the Lord?

_____

_____

_____

_____

_____

Probing the Depths

Satan is an enemy ever on the look-out for places within us where his poisonous thoughts and vicious lies can take root and grow into sin. He tempts us toward thoughts of self-sufficiency and independent ways. We must resist his attempts to lead us into the sin of pride; a sin that will defeat us more surely than any other.

However, one cannot simply resist satan with human strength and cause him to flee. One must first fully submit to God. This humbling or submission consists of godly sorrow and confession of sin, which results in a clean, undivided heart. It includes a recommitment to God of all areas of life so that one's hands (activities) are blameless. This humble placement under God is an act of worship which releases God's grace. God draws near, not only enabling the will to refuse satan's entice-ments, but also securing the victory as the Christian takes the offensive by resisting satan with the Word of God (Luke 4:1–13).

Satan lures us toward defeat by tempting the flesh to submit to his ways and use their own strength to get what they want. God calls us to depend on His grace working in and through us as the only way to victory. The Bible warns that exalting self will lead to a disgraceful fall, but humbling oneself leads to exaltation in this world and the next.

The life of peace founded upon humility and submission to God is true wisdom.

Read Proverbs 1:7; Luke 4:1–13; James 4:1–12.

Questions:

In what areas of your life do you find your greatest struggle with temptation?

✎ _____

_____

_____

_____

_____

What steps can you take to more effectively fight this temptation?

✎ _____

_____

_____

_____

The Response of a Humble Heart

Humility causes us to recognize our own severe limitations and great need. It compels us to reach beyond ourselves and to acknowledge that only in God can we find fulfillment and true life. That realization will ultimately fill our hearts with gratitude and thanksgiving that must find expression. That expression is praise to our Almighty God and Father.

Our God is worthy of our praise! Psalm 18:3 says, "I will call upon the Lord, who is worthy to be praised." The word translated as "praise" in this verse is the Hebrew *halal*. The most primitive meaning of this word is "to cause to shine." Thus, with our praise, we are throwing the spotlight on our God, who is worthy and deserves to be praised and glorified. The more we put the spotlight on Him, the more He causes us to shine.

Read Psalm 47; 50:23; 63:1–5; 22:3–5.

Questions:

The word translated "understanding" in Psalm 47:7 is the Hebrew *sakal* meaning prudent or cautious, leading to intelligence or wisdom. How can praising be wise?

_____

_____

_____

_____

What are the benefits of a life filled with humility and praise?

_____

_____

_____

_____

_____

Kingdom Extra

Read Psalm 24:3–5.

Few principles of Scripture are more essential to our understanding of Kingdom Dynamics than the powerful truth found in Psalm 22:3: the presence of God's kingdom power is directly related to the practice of God's praise. The verb "enthroned" indicates that wherever God's people exalt His name, He is ready to manifest His kingdom's power in the way most appropriate to the situation, as His rule is invited to invade our circumstance.

It is this fact that properly leads many to conclude that in a very real way, praise prepares a specific and present place for God among His people. Some have chosen the term "establish His throne" to describe this "enthroning" of God in our midst by our worshipping and praising welcome. God awaits the prayerful and praise-filled worship of His people as an entry point for His kingdom to "come"—to enter, that His "will be done" in human circumstances. We do not manipulate God, but align ourselves with the great kingdom truth: His is the power, ours is the privilege (and responsibility) to welcome Him into our world—our private, present world or the circumstances of our society.

Question:

What Scripture passages can you locate that support this understanding of the power of praise?

✎_____

_____

_____

_____

_____

An Attitude of Heart

Read Matthew 21:12–17, and listen as Jesus speaks of perfected praise.

In response to the criticism leveled against the powerful praise given Him, Jesus recalls the words of Psalm 8:2. However, rather than simply quoting the Psalms passage, Jesus reveals to us a powerful truth by interpreting the meaning of the Psalm: perfected praise will produce strength!

But, how is it that infants and babes perfect praise? And how can this lead to strength?

Consider the attributes of an infant. Of all people, a baby is the most trusting. All wants and needs must be supplied by another and there is no loss of self-esteem in their recognition of dependence. An infant is ever watchful to discover how to relate to life and learn the ways of the world into which they have been born. Ambition, greed, and ego are unknown in a baby's heart. There is no self-serving motive in their desire to learn and grow. When a baby turns his eyes toward a loving parent, the love, trust and complete dependence expressed can only be described as praise—devotion in its purest form.

The trust of a well-loved child is sure and that trust leads to the freedom to experience and grow. Knowing his safety rests in the one he adores, fear is far from the heart of a child. Children walk boldly into life with an insatiable desire to know and experience, looking to the one they love to teach them the way of life. Trust provides a child with the strength necessary to encounter all the unknowns of life and overcome the obstacles in the path to maturity.

If we could but operate in our relationship to the Lord as a child with a loving parent, we could walk free from fear and walk boldly with the strength which finds its source in the love of God. We would turn trusting eyes toward our loving, heavenly Father and express the truest praise—devotion from a heart filled with inexpressible love and unlimited trust.

Perfected praise will not only produce strength in our own lives; it will operate powerfully in situations. At the very moment when Jesus was being rejected by the religious and political leaders, the praise offered by children was more powerful than the circumstance. While the leaders attempted to cast doubt on Jesus' authority, the children were captivated by the sudden realization of who Jesus is. This revelation about Him brought forth loud and powerful praise. And it brought a sudden halt to the proceedings!

The psalms repeatedly remind us that "The Lord is the strength of my life."

Read Psalm 27:1; 46:1–3; 73:26; 118:14–19; Mark 10:13–16.

Questions:

In what ways do you see the attributes of "childlike devotion" in your own life?

✎_____

_____

_____

_____

In what ways is this degree of love and trust lacking?

✎_____

_____

_____

_____

What areas of your life are lacking in strength?

✎_____

_____

_____

_____

_____

Record Your Thoughts

Reread Psalm 47.

Questions:

Describe the relationship between humility and knowing God's nature.

✎_____

_____

_____

_____

_____

_____

What are the areas of your life where you struggle with pride?

✎_____

_____

_____

_____

_____

How are pride and an independent spirit related?

✎_____

_____

_____

_____

_____

_____

What steps can you take in your own life to develop a lifestyle of praise?

✎_____

_____

_____

_____

_____

_____

SESSION SIX

The Way of Submission
Psalm 50

Kingdom Key—*Listen and Obey*

Proverbs 4:4 Let your heart retain my words; keep my commands and live.

To submit is to willingly yield one's opinions in favor of another's; to be obedient to the voice of another. God has given us His word and in it has revealed His will for our lives: our behavior, our attitudes and our values. The power of God's word is released in us when we yield to Him by listening and obeying. Deuteronomy 28:1 says, "Now it shall come to pass, if you diligently obey the voice of the LORD your God, to observe carefully all His commandments which I command you today, that the LORD your God will set you high above all nations of the earth." What a fantastic promise to those who obey the Word of God!

Read Psalm 50:23; Proverbs 8:32–26; James 1:22–25; Romans 2:5–11; Philippians 2:5–8.

Questions:

Would you describe yourself as obedient to the will of God?

_____

_____

_____

Where is your obedience lacking?

_____

_____

_____

What steps might you take to improve your ability to surrender your will to God?

✎ _____

_____

_____

_____

_____

Kingdom Life—*The Authority of God's Word*

The Word of God is all-encompassing, absolutely authoritative, and forever, unchangingly secured in heaven. We can therefore know beyond doubt that: 1) Though times and seasons change, though social customs, human opinions, and philosophical viewpoints vary, they have no effect on the constancy or authority of God's Word. 2) God is faithful in applying the power, promise, and blessing of His Word, along with its requirements of justice and judgment. Just as He spoke and the Earth was created and is sustained, so He has spoken regarding His laws for living. The relativism of human thought does not affect His authority or standards. 3) While creation abides by His Word (responding as His "servants"), man is often a study in contrast to this submission to the Creator's authority. However, no matter the degree of our past rebellion, upon coming to Christ, a practical reinstatement of God's Word as the governing principle for all our life is to take place. As "spiritual" people we are to refuse the "natural" inclinations of fallen men. As we hear and yield to the authority of God's Word, we verify that we are no longer dominated by the world's spirit of error.

Read Psalm 19:7–11; John 8:47; 1 Corinthians 2:13–16; 1 John 4:6.

Questions:

How often do you read the Bible?

✎ _____

_____

_____

_____

In what ways do you allow the truths in Scripture to rule your life?

✎ _____

_____

_____

_____

Explain how you understand decision to be a key element in yielding to the authority of God's Word?

✎ _____

_____

_____

_____

Word Wealth—*Salvation*

Salvation: Greek *soteria* (so-tay-ree'-ah); Strong's #4991: Deliverance, preservation, soundness, prosperity, happiness, rescue, general well-being. The word is used in both a material, temporal sense and in a spiritual, eternal sense. The New Testament especially uses the word for spiritual well-being. Salvation is a present possession (Luke 1:77; 2 Corinthians 1:6; 7:10) with a fuller realization in the future (Romans 13:11; 1 Thessalonians 5:8, 9).

Kingdom Life—*Salvation Is Ours*

Jesus Christ is our salvation. He has provided us with deliverance from the bondage of sin and death. He has rescued us from destruction through his victorious resurrection. We have been "saved" by His overwhelming grace. Christ's salvation has not only secured our eternal home, but has provided the way to victorious living today, in the now of our lives.

Salvation is an event, a process, and a future occurrence. Christ enters our lives when we accept Him as our Savior. Through His work in us we are becoming what He created us to be; through His intercession for us all we need is supplied. Salvation in Christ has defeated the power of sin and death and reinstated our standing before the Father. It has provided for us the way to true, vibrant, abundant life; now as well as in the world to come.

Read Psalm 21:1–7; 27:1–2; 91:8; Luke 1:77; 2 Corinthians 1:6–10; Romans 13:1; 1 Thessalonians 5:8–9.

Question:

In what ways do you experience your present salvation?

_____

_____

_____

_____

Stand on the Promises

The promises of the Word of God cover every situation and circumstance we could possibly face. If we read the Word of God and understand God's will for our lives and the promises He has given us, then we can boldly face the future. God has given us the keys of His kingdom to unlock supernatural provisions for our lives by the power of His Word. Our responsibility is to know what His Word says and to ask God for what we need. We can overcome in this life if we take full advantage of the supernatural provisions that He has made available to us in Christ. We are specifically warned not to act as the Gentiles who are ignorant of God's provisions and spend all their time worrying and scheming about how to get ahead in life.

God is intimately concerned with every aspect of our lives. His Word covers provisions for not only our spiritual well-being, but our health, finances, marriage, career, sex life, and so on. Many in religious circles have had a tendency to overspiritualize the meaning of the word "salvation" and divorce it from the practical issues of life. But this is not what the Bible teaches. God, as a good heavenly Father, is not only concerned with our eternal salvation, but He is also concerned about our total well-being here on earth.

Read Psalm 119:41–45; Proverbs 13:13; 16:20; Philippians 4:19; Malachi 3:10; James 5:14–15; Acts 1:8.

Questions:

What are some of the provisions God has given us in order to enable us to live abundantly in the here and now?

✎_____

_____

_____

_____

Locate other Scripture passages that reveal God's present provision for you.

✎_____

_____

_____

_____

What practical steps of obedience are required to posses these provisions?

✎_____

_____

_____

_____

Meditate and Move Out

Unlike Eastern meditation, which encourages emptying of the mind and a general passivity, when the Bible speaks about meditating on the Word of God, it means constantly thinking about a particular passage of Scripture and gleaning all the great truths it contains. This may involve opening a Bible, reading a particular verse or passage over and over again, and asking God to reveal its meaning to you. It may involve shutting out all other thoughts except for a Bible verse and shutting ourselves up before God so that we can hear His voice.

But we must not merely read the Word, we must act on what we have learned. The power of God's Word is fully released in our lives when we obey and do what the Word of God says. The power of God's Word is released and activated through faith and obedience.

Read Psalm 119:15–16, 26–27; James 1:22; Matthew 7:21–28.

Questions:

Do you regularly meditate on God's Word?

_____

_____

_____

_____

What is the result?

_____

_____

_____

_____

Kingdom Life—*Humility Leads to Obedience*

Nowhere is the mind of Christ presented to the Christian more strongly than in Philippians 2:1–11. Appealing to the Philippians to be of "one mind" in pursuing humility, Paul cites the example of the incarnation of God in Jesus Christ. Paul urges us to take on the mind of Christ. Unlike Adam, who sought to be equal with God (Genesis 3:5), Christ did not try to grasp for equality with God. Instead, being God, He poured Himself out and took upon Himself the form of a slave, to the point of dying the death of a common criminal. "Therefore," glories Paul, "God . . . has highly exalted Him, and given Him the name which is above every name" (2:9).

This is the Christ whose attitude and intention all believers must share. To be identified with Christ in humility and obedience is the noblest achievement to which anyone can aspire.

Read Proverbs 16:18–19; 22:4; Psalm 25:9–10; Philippians 2:1–1; James 4:10.

Questions:

How does humility look in your own life?

_____

_____

_____

_____

How has this affected your obedience to God?

_____

_____

_____

_____

Word Wealth—*Obedience*

Obedience: Greek, *hupakoe* (hoop-ak-o-ay'); Strong's #5218: From *hupo* meaning under and *akouo* which means to hear or listen. The word signifies attentive hearing, listening with compliant submission, assent, and agreement. It is used for obedience in general, for obedience to God's commands, and for Christ's obedience.

Yield to God

Obedience to God is the ultimate form of yielding to Him. Scripture tells us that to "obey is better than sacrifice." Giving over our will has more life-changing power than the relinquishing of any possession or faculty. Obedience is the recognition of God's supreme authority. We yield readily to God when we recognize His pre-eminence and our own sinful inability to live righteously before Him.

In order to obey, we must be aware of those things God requires of us and be equipped by Him to comply with His commands. We can learn of His desires for us only from Him.

Read Proverbs 4; 1 Samuel 15:22, 23a; Psalm 50:23.

Questions:

How and where do we learn of God's commands and His will for our lives?

✎_____

_____

_____

_____

_____

How does God equip us to obey?

✎_____

_____

_____

_____

_____

What is God's promise to those who obey His commands?

✎_____

_____

_____

_____

_____

How does obedience lead to freedom?

✎_____

_____

_____

_____

_____

Record Your Thoughts

Reread Psalm 50.

Questions:

What changes can you make in your life that will reflect the importance of knowing God's will?

✎ _____

_____

_____

_____

_____

_____

_____

For the next two weeks, set aside 15 minutes from every day to simply sit quietly before the Lord and let Him speak to you from His Word. Keep a journal of what you hear.

✎ _____

_____

_____

_____

_____

_____

_____

What about this session has most impacted your view of submission?

✎ _____

_____

_____

_____

_____

_____

_____

ADDITIONAL OBSERVATIONS

SESSION SEVEN

The Way of Stewardship
Psalm 90

Kingdom Key—*Act Honorably*

Proverbs 10:5 He who gathers in summer is a son who acts wisely, but he who sleeps in harvest is a son who acts shamefully.

The Bible gives us clear guidelines for the wise and careful use of the many gifts God has bestowed upon us. Being disciplined with regard to our time, material wealth, minds, and bodies is results in a life that brings glory to the One we serve and paves the way in our own lives for greater blessing.

The believer's stewardship incorporates accountability for the way in which he or she manages life's affairs as given into their care. The care of the matters of one's "house" includes personal responsibility to private duties, attention to one's family and its obligations, pursuit of vocational tasks and scope of influence, service to God by serving human need, and use of appropriate opportunities to extend the kingdom. These are accomplished through the faithful stewardship of one's monies, time, abilities, and influence.

Read Psalm 90:12; Malachi 3:8–12; Matthew 25:14–40; Hebrews 3:2; Luke 12:13–26; Luke 6:38; 2 Corinthians 8:1–9, 15.

Questions:

How do you understand the plea of the psalmist, "teach us to number our days?"

_____

_____

Do you see yourself as a "wise steward?"

✎ _____

_____

In what ways do you "invest" what God has entrusted to your care?

✎ _____

_____

_____

_____

What steps can you take to increase your accountability in these areas?

✎ _____

_____

_____

_____

Kingdom Life—*Time Is Short, Use It Well*

This life is so very fleeting. When we are young, it seems time is limitless; but as we age we learn the inescapable truth that our days on earth are numbered and will soon pass into eternity. The brevity of life demands conscientious stewardship from one who would be a faithful servant. In meditating upon human frailty, Moses compared life to grass that withers. God Himself, on the other hand, is from everlasting to everlasting.

Because of sin, God has shortened man's time at least twice. We learn in Genesis that the early days of man averaged hundreds of years: Seth, for example, lived 912 years, and Methuselah, 969 years. After the Flood however, God shortened man's time to 120 years. When we reach the time represented in Psalm 90, man's years have been cut to seventy or eighty years. Your life is a vapor, with no guarantee as to the number of your years. Therefore, it is critical that you allow God to teach you to manage well the brief time you have here.

Read Psalm 90:1–17; Proverbs 19:15, 31:27; James 4:13–16; 2 Thessalonians 3:10.

Questions:

In what ways do you make the most of the time you have in regard to:

Relationships?

✎ _____

_____

_____

_____

Service?

✎ _____

_____

_____

_____

The pursuit of knowing God?

✎ _____

_____

_____

_____

In what ways to you tend to idle away your time?

✎ _____

_____

_____

_____

How does this steal from the godly riches you might otherwise attain?

✎ _____

_____

_____

_____

_____

Where Is Your Heart?

Jesus told us that our heart will be committed to those things we treasure most. It is a sad truth that money and possessions hold the heart of many who profess that their commitment is to our Lord. Money and possessions can exert a crippling hold on those who have fallen prey to its empty promises and lies. This is not a disease peculiar to the current time, but has been prevalent in the hearts of men since sin entered the world.

Read Proverbs 11:4–6, Psalm 19:14; 26:2–12; 22:4, 30:7–9; Matthew 6:19–21.

Questions:

Take an honest look at your heart where money and possessions are concerned.

✎ _____

_____

_____

_____

In what ways have these things taken over your heart?

✎ _____

_____

_____

_____

If values are expressed by the amount of time devoted, what does your life tell others you value most?

✎ _____

_____

_____

_____

What steps can you take to align your priorities with the Word of God?

✎ _____

_____

_____

_____

Kingdom Life—*Tithing Is for Today*

Tithing is the practice of giving a tenth of one's income or property as an offering to God. The custom of paying a tithe is a timeless practice established as a part of believing worship.

Some New Testament believers decry tithing as relevant to Old Testament Law, and thus contrary to the law of liberty and grace. The first recorded tithe occurs in Genesis and Jesus Himself spoke of tithing as relevant to believers. Tithing was instituted by God for a purpose. That purpose is just as living and applicable today as in Old Testament times. God's Word reveals that *all* His blessings and covenants are of grace, not law.

The Bible clearly reveals tithing as a divinely ordered, financial discipline with wonderful promises to follow; promises that are guaranteed by God Himself. God does not make a legal demand, declaring that if we don't tithe, we will not go to heaven. Salvation's promise transcends legalistic demands. But there is a principle of tithing and giving which God has wrapped into the very structure of creation. Just as the law of gravity manifests predictable responses in the created universe, so does giving or its absence manifest effects in the spiritual realm—and practical outflow of our spiritual responses. Thus, when redeemed humans learn to *let go,* to *give,* to *release,* room is made for life and abundance to flow into their lives according to God's order.

Nothing will keep a wise believer from tithing and giving, but he or she will never be found to tithe or give offerings just to get something in return. Rather, the act arises from obedience, and God always rewards obedience!

Read Psalm 96:7–8; Haggai 1:6; Malachi 3:10; Matthew 23:23; Luke 6:38.

Questions:

What is your opinion of tithing?

✎_____

_____

_____

_____

_____

What does this say of your understanding that all things are provided by God and are to be used to serve Him?

✎_____

_____

_____

_____

_____

 **Probing the Depths—*Why Do Some Suffer Want?***

Poverty severely handicaps many people. Poverty can be caused by disobedience to the Word. Those who withhold their tithes and offerings are, in a very real way, robbing God. As a consequence, they are also robbing themselves of the blessings that God wants to bestow upon them.

God always acts in accordance with the laws and principles that He has established in the world. One facet of God's commitment to those principles is that He will never violate man's right to choose and act independently from His will and plan. While God is above man's choices and actions, His actions never violate the reality of human choice. Sinful acts do occur and the result is life outside God's plan. The consequence of one man's sin can be far reaching and may touch innocent lives.

Poverty can come as a result of the horrors of war, because of unjust or unwise government, because of oppression by the greedy and the ruthless, sometimes because of disobedience to God's commandments, and sometimes because of lack of knowledge of God's principles of blessing. Sometimes temporary poverty follows a satanic attack or a serious and unexplainable calamity.

Poverty and want exist, even in the lives of the ones who love and serve the Lord. But a heart that is wholly committed to the Lord will trust Him, regardless of circumstance. They can find contentment that transcends their situation. They can enter into that place of rest that Paul experienced when he said, "I have learned in whatever state I am, to be content: I know how to be abased, and I know how to abound. Everywhere and in all things I have learned both to be full and to be hungry, both to abound and to suffer need. I can do all things through Christ who strengthens me."

To more fully understand this issue of poverty, locate other Scriptures that clarify God's providence. It may be of great value to locate a good commentary or Bible handbook to assist you in your search.

The Lifestyle of a Good Steward

A chosen lifestyle reflects those things that are valued and those standards that are adopted. It is lived out in body and mind showing the world what we consider to have worth and importance.

Many Christians live defeated lives by yielding to the flesh, which seemingly has a will of its own. The flesh poses endless challenges to a lifestyle of honor and stewardship. A truly honorable life is made possible when Christians present both spirit and body to Christ. The believer's lifestyle is his reasonable service. Our bodies and minds are not ours to defile with willful acts of sins. We must recognize that a life given over to the service of our Lord is sacrificial and that the Christian lifestyle is holy—not worldly, but God-conscious and God-centered. Nothing else is acceptable to God.

Christians must be nonconformists to the systems of this world. We should not conform to this world because we are not of this world. A servant of the Lord Jesus should rather be transformed by a renewed mind. The worldly conform to the fads and customs of the times as seen and passed on by media campaigns. The believer's mind is renewed by adherence to God's Word.

Read Psalm 90:14–17; Proverbs 8:17–21; Romans 11:33—12:2.

Questions:

What is the wealth that is promised by God to those who diligently seek Him?

_____
_____
_____
_____
_____
_____

What is a transformed mind? In what ways does your life reflect this?

_____
_____
_____

What impact will a life of sacrificial service to God have on your relationships with those the Lord has placed in your life?

_____
_____
_____
_____
_____

Record Your Thoughts

Questions:

How are stewardship and an honorable lifestyle related?

_____

_____

_____

_____

What mindset is behind a lifestyle of good stewardship?

_____

_____

_____

_____

_____

What are God's promises to those who manage His gifts honorably?

_____

_____

_____

_____

_____

Do you experience the outworking of those promises in your life? Why do you believe this is so?

_____

_____

_____

_____

_____

ADDITIONAL OBSERVATIONS

The Way of Confidence

Psalm 94

 Kingdom Life—*Rely on God*

Proverbs 3:25–26 Do not be afraid of sudden fear, nor of the onslaught of the wicked when it comes; for the Lord will be your confidence, and will keep your foot from being caught.

To rely means to be totally dependent upon or completely confident in, based on experience. In no other instance and in no other relationship is this word more correctly used than in our relationship to God. He alone can grant life and blessing. God is our source of all good things. He alone is capable of keeping us in safety. We can rest securely knowing we are held by love in His mighty hand.

However, worry, anxiety, and fear are emotional states that plague our society. If our confidence is based on ourselves or any of society's sanctuaries (government, corporations, economy, and the like) insecurity and worry are inevitable. As children of the kingdom, our confidence is to be found in the Lord, not in the futile ways of man. We can rely on our God, knowing that His hand is not short and His power is never constrained. He alone holds the answers and the power. He alone can free us from worry, anxiety, and fear.

Read Psalm 94:19; Proverbs 1:33; 1 Corinthians 18–23; Luke 12:22–32.

Questions:

In what ways do you experience worry, fear, or anxiety in your own life?

How are worry fear and anxiety related? What do they have in common?

✎ _____

_____

_____

_____

How might a greater reliance upon God alleviate or put an end to these fears?

✎ _____

_____

_____

_____

_____

 Word Wealth—*Futile*

Futile: Greek *mataioo* (mat-ah-yah´-oh); Strong's #3154: To make empty, vain, foolish, useless, confused. The word describes the perverted logic and idolatrous presumptions of those who do not honor God or show Him any gratitude for His blessings on humanity.

Trust Beyond Reason

The word translated as "confidence" in our Kingdom Key Proverb implies the idea of trust without need of thought or consideration. At its root, it literally means silly or foolish.

In 1 Corinthians 1:26–31, Paul tells us that God has chosen the foolish things of the world to put to shame the wise. To the world, the trust and confidence we have in God seems foolishness. But those who know Him in the power of His love, will trust even when it seems the world holds no answer for us. When reason demands defeat, faith will expect victory. We can stand sure in the knowledge that God will ever come to the aid of those who serve Him.

Read Psalm 103:1–5; Proverbs 10:3; 12:28; Matthew 11:25–30.

Questions:

With what do you struggle most in times of trial?

_____

_____

_____

_____

_____

How would having confidence in God change this?

_____

_____

_____

_____

_____

Kingdom Life—*Ask Then Rest*

It can be extremely difficult to rest in faith, believing God cares about our needs. Interaction with a fallen world hinders our ability to trust and our view of God is often colored by our experience. Even when we pray, we may have trouble believing God is listening and will answer when we call. To make matters worse, the enemy of our prayer life will even attempt to deceive us into fearing that. Not only will our needs **not** be met, but something worse will happen. He will whisper, "You will get what you deserve." But as you allow the truth of God's Word to shape your thinking, you will find yourself enabled to rest while believing that your loving Father will hear your pleas and will respond by supplying your needs. Faith will rise in the confidence that God your Father—who has revealed Himself in the person of His Son Jesus Christ—will give *only good things* to His children; only blessing, not cursing, to those who pray to Him in faith.

Read Psalm 94:12–13; Proverbs 10:24, 28; Matthew 7:7–11; Luke 11:9–13.

Questions:

Describe the life you believe God desires for His people in this world.

_____

_____

_____

_____

_____

In what way does your life fail to reflect this?

_____

_____

_____

_____

What steps can you take to remedy this?

_____

_____

_____

_____

_____

Word Wealth—*Faith*

Faith: Greek *pistis* (pis'-tis); Strong's #4102: Conviction, confidence, trust, belief, reliance, trustworthiness, and persuasion. In the New Testament setting, *pistis* is the divinely implanted principle of inward confidence, assurance, trust, and reliance in God and all that He says. It can refer to the body of truth that we believe (1 Timothy 1:19), to the basic trust we have in God for salvation (Ephesians 2:8) or to the dynamic power which realizes the energy contained in the promises of God. As a dynamic power, faith is an agency for action; it is this aspect which best describes the 1 Corinthians manifestation.

Kingdom Extra—*Confidence in Trial*

Even though we believe God and follow His Word and way, we have no guarantee against times of lack and hardship. Our journey of faith will undoubtedly pass through times of trial and loss. Sometimes these places of hardship come in the form of lost jobs, sickness, or one of a multitude of ways that suffering can enter our lives.

Our society suggests that the experience of victory over any hardship can only be real when you have *what* you want *when* you want it. But the Bible teaches that you win, not when you get what you want, but *the moment you believe!* If I'm surrounded by problems, I win *not* when they're solved, but the moment I believe God's promise that He'll sustain me through or beyond it. If I am sick, I win over sickness; not when I get well, but the moment I believe in God's promises which make Jesus Christ the Healer alive and real to me. If I find myself in poverty, I win the moment I believe what He has said about my financial circumstances. You and I are overcomers the moment we place our faith in the Son of God, and what His Word is speaking into our lives.

Faith should not be understood as the power to ward off evil. Faith is the God-given power to process reality. Faith never denies reality but moves through it in confidence toward God's promise of victory. Read Psalm 94:21–22; 1 John 5:4.

Questions:

Consider the times of trial in your own life.

_____

_____

_____

What has been your reaction?

_____

_____

_____

_____

How would relying on God have changed your outlook? How might it have changed the situation?

✎ _____

_____

_____

_____

The Glory of Hardship

The whole created universe has suffered the consequences of human sin, being subjected to the process of deterioration. In our lives this is experienced as suffering and loss. Although our souls are assured salvation and eternal reward, our bodies are still subject to pain and sin.

However, even in hardship and suffering, even in bitter disappointments, even when wrongly treated, Christians can know that God will work amidst such situations to fulfill His good purpose in His children. The situation may or may not be directly changed by God, but even if situations remain difficult God guarantees ultimate good results, including the maturation of the character of His child.

God is changing us, maturing us so that we reflect the life and person of Jesus. That change often takes place in the midst of hardship and trial. When we recognize our own inability to affect change in our circumstance or in our own heart, we more fully recognize our dependence upon God. When we see our own weakness, we learn to rely on His strength, His wisdom and His direction.

We will undoubtedly experience times of discouragement, but the assurance of Christ's present love, active at every moment of life, will override despair and lead us to victory. We may remain in the circumstance, but sure knowledge of the love of Christ will keep us secure even when the world around lies in chaos and ruin.

We are Christians, the Christ-like ones. We are to live as He lived and our path will lead us along the path He walked—from suffering to glory. Our status as children of God guarantees our participation in the present and future joy of God's kingdom. We may experience temporary sorrow, but joy will most certainly come.

Read Psalm 30:5–12; Romans 8:27–39; 2 Corinthians 3:16–18.

Questions:

Have you ever experienced a trial that caused you to doubt God's love?

✐ _____

_____

_____

_____

What happened as a result?

✐ _____

_____

_____

What things have happened in your life that give proof that God's love will sustain you in any circumstance?

✐ _____

_____

_____

_____

Record Your Thoughts

Reread Psalm 94.

Questions:

Tell of the ways you have experienced the Lord upholding you during times of trial?

✐ _____

_____

_____

_____

God is our defense and refuge. Tell what this means to you.

✎ _____

_____

_____

_____

_____

_____

How have you experienced this in your own life?

✎ _____

_____

_____

_____

_____

_____

The Way of Courage
Psalm 112

 Kingdom Key—*Find Strength in the Lord*

Proverbs 14:26 In the fear of the Lord there is strong confidence, and his children will have a place of refuge.

Every true child of God soon learns that the Christian life is a life of warfare. The hosts of satan are committed to hinder and obstruct the work of Christ and to knock the individual soldier out of combat. The more effective a believer is for the Lord, the more he will experience the savage attacks of the enemy: the devil does not waste his ammunition on nominal Christians. In our own strength we are no match for the devil. If we are to stand against the attacks of our enemy, we must be continually strengthened in the Lord and in the boundless resources of His might. God's best soldiers are those who are conscious of their own weakness and ineffectiveness, and who rely solely on Him. Our weakness commends itself to the power of His might.

Read Psalm 112:7–8; Proverbs 10:29; Ephesians 6:10–18.

Questions:

How can we find strength in the Lord?

_____

_____

_____

_____

When have you experienced this in your own life?

_____

_____

_____

_____

Victorious Thinking

Just walking from day to day will confirm the reality of the war we face. We are in engaged in a spiritual warfare against an enemy who wishes to destroy us.

Weapons are employed by opposing sides in every war. Spiritual warfare is no different. Satan's most potent weapon is often against our minds. He wages concentrated attacks aimed at confusing our thoughts and leading us toward conclusions that are flawed and defeating.

God has given us weapons with which to engage in effective battle against our enemy. These weapons do not arise out of our humanity. Even the most brilliant, resourceful, and strongest among us cannot overcome the enemy with whom we battle. But our weapons are divine. Since they come from God, they are more powerful than anything the enemy brings against us. They are sufficient to destroy every fortress of evil we encounter.

What is our responsibility in this war? Very simply, we are, by God's power, to take control of our minds, our thought life. What was true of the original temptation and fall in the garden is still true today. Our minds (hearts, emotions, and will), represent the real battleground between the two kingdoms within our lives as believers. That is the testimony of the entire New Testament confirmed by victorious daily experience. If we win the battle in our own minds, we have won the war. The battle Adam and Eve lost is reenacted almost daily in the mind and heart of every child of God; thus the importance given in Scripture to the mind and to its almost equivalent term, the heart.

Read Psalm 112:6–8; Proverbs 23:7; 2 Corinthians 10:3–5.

Questions:

What do you understand "his heart is established" to mean?

_____

_____

_____

_____

_____

How can an established heart set the scene for victory in the battle of the mind?

_____

_____

_____

_____

_____

_____

Probing the Depths

For nearly all of us, there are strongholds—places where satan has so hindered us and confused our thinking that we seem helpless to find victory in battling them. These strongholds are first established in the mind; that is why we are to take every thought captive. Behind a stronghold is also a lie—a place of personal bondage where God's Word has been subjugated to any unscriptural idea or personally confused belief that is held to be true. Behind every lie is a fear, and behind every fear is an idol. Idols are established wherever there exists a failure to trust in the provisions of God that are ours through Jesus Christ. Some of the weapons that pull down these strongholds are: God's Word, the blood of the Cross, and the name of Jesus. Strongholds are pulled down and confronted bondage is broken as these spiritual weapons of our warfare are employed.

Read Psalm 112:1; Proverbs 7:1–2; Hebrews 4:12, 13; Mark 16:17; Revelation 12:11; Ephesians 6:13–18.

Questions:

What strongholds exist in your life?

✎ _____

_____

_____

_____

What steps can you take to find freedom from this bondage?

✎ _____

_____

_____

_____

Word Wealth—*Refuge*

Refuge: Hebrew *machseh* (mahch-seh'); Strong's #4268: A shelter, refuge, protection, fortress; a hope; a place of trust; a shelter from the storm. This noun occurs 20 times in the Old Testament, more than half of these is in the Psalms. *Machseh* is also translated as trust (Psalm 73:78), where the psalmist has put his trust in the Lord; he has made the Lord his trustworthy place of shelter.

He Is Our Very Present Help

Read Psalm 46.

The Lord will aid us in times of trouble. His faithfulness has been tried throughout the ages and He has never failed. He has ever been a place of refuge for His children and He has never allowed their enemies to have the final victory. No present or future calamity should give us reason to fear. No matter what our eyes report, our heart should rest securely in the ability of our God to protect and the strength of His arm to save.

In contrast to what may be a raging environment around us there is a peaceful river that flows from the throne of God. Within that river is a limitless flow of supply that produces life. This unseen river is a symbol of the inner life, grace, and joy that only complete trust in God gives. We have no reason to fear any circumstance, power or authority because our Father is over them all. We only need focus our eyes on Him and the reality of His dominion.

We dwell in safety and free from all fear when we recognize that our God *is* God and His love for us knows no bounds.

Questions:

What does Psalm 112 have to say in this regard?

✎_____

_____

_____

_____

Are you convinced of God's love for you?

✎_____

_____

_____

_____

With this Scripture in mind, what could cause fear in the heart of a Christian?

✎_____

_____

_____

_____

Find other Scriptures that proclaim God's love for us and His intention to be our "refuge and strength."

✎_____

_____

_____

_____

Word Wealth—*Fear*

Fear: Greek *phobos* (fob'-oss); Strong's #5401: In classical Greek the word signified flight. Later it came to denote that which causes flight; hence, fear, terror, dread. The English word "phobia" transliterates the Greek word *phobos*.

Kingdom Life—*We Can Be Fearless*

Christianity gave love (Greek *agape*) a new meaning. This word rarely occurs in existing non-biblical Greek manuscripts written during the period of the New Testatment. *Agape* denotes an undefeatable benevolence and unconquerable good-will that always seeks the highest good of the other person, no matter what he does. It is the selfless love that gives freely, without asking anything in return, and does not consider the worth of its object. *Agape* is a love by choice, and it refers to the will to love rather than the emotion of love. *Agape* describes the unconditional love God has for the world.

His love for the world and toward each of us is complete. Fear grips our souls because we are more convinced of the triumph of circumstance and sin over us than the undefeatable, unconquerable love that securely holds us. We are His and He finds us precious.

Today He will keep us in His love, and if we will hold tightly to Him, He will drive our fears far from us.

Read Psalms 112:6–8; Proverbs 8:17–35; 1 John 4:17–19.

Questions:

When do you doubt the Lord's love for you?

How does doubting the Lord's love negatively affect your walk of faith?

_____

_____

_____

_____

Record Your Thoughts

Reread Psalm 112.

Questions:

What does Scripture mean when it tells us that when we are weak, He is strong?

_____

_____

_____

What must we understand before we can truly walk in His strength?

_____

_____

_____

What does a courageous Christian look like?

_____

_____

_____

_____

Where is your courage lacking?

_____

_____

_____

_____

ADDITIONAL OBSERVATIONS

SESSION TEN

The Way of Peace
Psalm 127

 Kingdom Key—*Trust in God*

Proverbs 24:3–4 Through wisdom a house is built, and by understanding it is established; by knowledge the rooms are filled with all precious and pleasant riches.

We have already discovered that true prosperity is much more an internal response than an external state. A sure and certain peace is found at the very core of prosperity. This peace cannot be earned or acquired through human effort. It is the gift of God to a trusting heart.

Peaceful Christians emit peaceful "vibes"; people around them can perceive the residence of the Prince of Peace in their beings, in their lives. Peaceful Christians are content, not angry or frustrated, able to really *trust* God in all events of life. Joy is the external exhibition of inner peace (well-being and hopefulness), the demonstration of the life of contentment enjoyed by Christians who do not strive with life and God, but who rest in His provision and trust Him to supply.

Read Psalm 29:1; 127:1–2; Proverbs 3:33; 19:23; Philippians 4:7; John 16:33.

Questions:

How can you experience peace regardless of the circumstances of life?

What does a peaceful spirit tell others about our Lord?

✎ _____

_____

_____

_____

What does your attitude and outlook tell others about our Lord?

✎ _____

_____

_____

_____

Word Wealth—*Establish*

Establish: Hebrew *qûwm* (koom); Strong's #6965: to be fixed or certain; implies prosperity and faithfulness. *Qûwm* communicates the idea of a thing that has been prepared, confirmed, set in motion. It also contains the idea of a full and abundant realization and enduring reality. A "house" established through and by God will stand strong and certain; it will prosper and experience faithful, abundant provision.

Kingdom Life—*Trust the Architect*

Building a home is a painstaking endeavor. It begins with the architect who develops a plan. Skilled craftsmen and gifted artisans blend their handiwork and, by careful attention to the architects plans, create a beautiful, sound, long-lasting structure; a structure to house life and living, to offer refuge and protection, to be a home. It all begins with a plan developed by an architect with vision for what can be.

God the master builder knows how to build our lives, our spiritual homes. He is the architect. He developed the plan. His design is perfect and eternal. When we try to build our homes or our families without consulting the chief architect, our labor is in vain. But when we work with Him in the construction process, when we consult His blueprints—the Word of God—and seek His guidance in prayer, the result is an enduring refuge.

Read Psalm 127:1; Proverbs 12:7; 19:23; Matthew 7:24–27; 1 Peter 2:4–5.

Questions:

How do you understand the term "house" as it applies to the work of God in your life?

✎ _____

_____

_____

_____

If your life is a house, what are the areas that lack structural integrity?

✎ _____

_____

_____

_____

What steps can you take to build up these areas of your life?

✎ _____

_____

_____

_____

Living Stones

God is not only building our lives into spiritual "houses" wherein He is worshipped and glorified, but He is building a supernatural structure wherein the Holy Spirit dwells.

In the first letter of Peter, Jesus is referred to as "the living stone" and further identified as the cornerstone or capstone—a massive, foundational stone around which the walls of a structure are joined or the center stone which gives an arch its stability. Jesus is the supreme, most fundamental element in the spiritual house being built and established by God on earth—the church. He is the pre-eminent "living stone."

Likewise all believers are "living stones" in the earthly dwelling place of God's glory.

Just as a physical structure, a home, is created to provide protection and security, so it is with the church.

Read Exodus 15:2; Psalm 131:13–16; Ephesians 2:19–22; 1 Peter 2:4–10.

Questions:

What are the qualities of a "living stone" in God's kingdom?

✑_____

_____

_____

How do we enter into this building process in preparing a habitation for God?

✑_____

_____

_____

Based on the analogy of "living stones," describe the relationship that should exist between Christ and the believer.

✑_____

_____

_____

Based on this analogy, what should characterize the relationships among believers.

✑_____

_____

_____

Word Wealth—*Church*

Church: Greek, *ecclesia* (ek-klay-see'-ah); Strong's #1577: The dominant use in the NT is to describe an assembly or company of Christians in the following ways: 1) the whole body of Christians; 2) a local church constituting a company of Christians gathering for worship, sharing, and teaching; 3) churches in a district. Other related terms are: "spiritual house," "chosen race," and "God's people." (Compare "ecclesiastic" and "ecclesiastical.")

The Household of Faith

It is Jesus' intent to establish the "community of the king." This community is His church. Although He spoke infrequently about the church (only in Matthew 16 and 18), His emphasis on the kingdom implies an ongoing realm within which His will is done and His rule is honored. In Galatians, this community is referred to as the "household of faith."

We are given many guidelines and directives as how to live within this "household." Nowhere are these guidelines more fitly spoken than by Paul in his letter to the Philippians. When faced with two women who were at odds, Paul pointed the way toward unity. After a call to earnest, extended prayer, Paul charged them to meditate on things positive, noble and praiseworthy. However, it was not his intent that these women simply fill their minds with pleasant thoughts, but to be so transformed in their thinking that their actions would naturally follow suit. Character and conduct begin in the mind. Actions are affected by the meditations of the heart.

Paul's guarantee to these women was that the result of prayerful, changed living would be peace that surpasses all understanding.

Read Psalm 34:14; 85:8–13; Proverbs 12:20; Philippians 4:2–9; Galatians 6:10; Colossians 3:12–17.

Questions:

How would you characterize your relationship with the Body of Christ?

✎ _____

_____

_____

_____

_____

_____

How can we choose the way of peace: internally and with others?

✎ _____

_____

_____

 Behind the Scenes

The yearning for unity is nearly universal. It is expressed in the motto "E Pluribus Unum" (out of many, one) of the United States. It is found in similar mottoes in other countries, and even in their names (United Kingdom, United Arab Emirates, the former Union of Soviet Socialist Republics). Even the name given to the international organization of nations pledged to promote peace and security around the world reflects this desire—the United Nations.

Our own families, like the family of nations, yearn for such unity as well. This yearning comes from God Himself who created us in His image to reflect His unity here on earth. If God created this universal yearning, whether national or personal, can He not fulfill it? Indeed He can! Indeed He is . . . in *His* family! The church is a "preview of coming attractions" when all things shall be united in Christ (Ephesians 1:9, 10). All that sin has disrupted; grace shall unite. And this process of making "out of many, one" begins with becoming "one" with the Lord through forgiveness of sin based on Christ's "at-one-ment" on the Cross. It continues through becoming "one" in heart and mind with brothers and sisters in Christ, especially those within our immediate family: husbands and wives, parents and children.

Read John chapter 17.

Questions:

What do you experience in your local church that personifies Jesus' prayer?

✎ _____

_____

_____

What do you experience that is contrary to Jesus' desire for His church?

✎ _____

_____

_____

_____

Kingdom Life—*Live in Peace*

Stress seems to be a constant companion of most in this hectic, pressurized world we inhabit. The natural human desires for acceptance, status, and possessions create tension; and the fear of either not attaining or losing our desires can cause anxiety and stress.

Managing stress for a Christian begins with understanding yourself and knowing what Scripture teaches about the nature of God. To understand yourself means to know your basic nature, the potential of your strengths, and the limits of your weaknesses. This is no small task, for self-deception can prevent clear discernment and pride and independence can block self-awareness. God Himself must give the self-awareness needed. Only He can show clearly where change is needed and bring about that change in basic human nature.

An understanding of the nature of God comes from His self-revelation in Scripture and in Christ. Understanding the quality of God's character inspires trust. Knowing, accepting and resting in His unchanging nature produces stability and peace.

Stress will dissipate and peace will reign when we acknowledge our dependence upon God and submit to His leadership. We are locked into time and space as finite creatures, while God is infinite, eternal, and omnipresent. He knows the beginning from the end and the path that will lead us to fulfillment and prosperity.

It is only through recognition of God's constant care and unlimited power that we begin on the pathway to peace. By trusting our lives to Him in prayer, submitting our desires to Him in supplication, and relinquishing our pride in thanksgiving, that we can realize a "peace . . .

which surpasses all understanding." We can rest securely knowing that we are the beloved children of our Father and He will always meet our needs.

Read Psalm 127:1–2; 139:23, 24; 73:26; 1 Peter 5:6, 7; Philippians 4:6–7.

Questions:

What causes you stress and worry in your life?

_____

_____

_____

_____

What does Solomon mean by "the Lord guards the city" in Psalm 127?

_____

_____

_____

_____

What impact would recognizing that God "guards the city" and "gives His beloved" all good things make in the stress points of your life?

_____

_____

_____

_____

How can peace guard your heart and mind?

_____

_____

_____

_____

Word Wealth—*Peace*

Peace: Hebrew *shalom* (shah-loam'); Strong's #7965: Completeness, wholeness, peace, health, welfare, safety, soundness, tranquility, prosperity, perfectness, fullness, rest, harmony; the absence of agitation or discord. *Shalom* comes from the root word *shalam*, meaning "to be complete, perfect, and full." This *shalom* is much more than the absence of conflict, it is the wholeness that the entire human race seeks. In Isaiah 53:5, the chastisement necessary to bring us *shalom* was upon the suffering Messiah. The angels understood at His birth that Jesus was to be the great peace-bringer, as they called out "Glory to God in the highest: and in earth peace, goodwill toward men!"

Peace: Greek *eirene* (eye-ray'-nay); Strong's #1515: A state of rest, quietness, and calmness; an absence of strife; tranquility. It generally denotes harmonious relationship with self, and between God and man, interpersonally, among nations, and within families. Jesus is the Prince of Peace. The Holy Spirit mediates the state of peace when the fruit of the Spirit is active, effective and affective in the hearts of persons.

Record Your Thoughts

Read Psalm 127 and 91.

Questions:

How does trusting God result in peace?

✎ _____

_____

_____

_____

What relationship does prayer have to "peace . . . that passes understanding?"

✎ _____

_____

_____

_____

What changes would need to happen in your life for you to experience true peace?

_____

_____

_____

_____

_____

_____

What are the similarities between an earthly family and the family of God?

_____

_____

_____

_____

_____

How can our spiritual "quiver" be full?

_____

_____

_____

_____

_____

The Way of Contentment

Psalm 128

 Kingdom Key—*Accept God's Rule*

Proverbs 19:23 The fear of the Lord leads to Life, so that one may sleep satisfied, untouched by evil.

Reaching the blessed state of satisfaction and contentment is not an easy task. Satisfaction when you have very real unmet needs, freedom from worry when you have overwhelming concerns, patience in letting God work when pressures abound—these seem like impossible dreams. Happiness—despite heartaches caused by the past, in the midst of tragedies experienced in the present, based on promises trusted for the future—is not merely a human pursuit but demands spiritual resources only found in the indwelling Holy Spirit.

God chose not to give you contentment as a gift. He chose rather to teach you to be content as you allow Him to be ruler in your life. Contentment is learned. As you trust God's gifts to be sufficient and His assignments to be appropriate, you can rest in circumstances of your life, knowing God will never fail you.

You must trust that God has given you everything needed for this moment in time. With that trust, you will be enabled to be content with yourself, your family, your surroundings, your job, and your past. As you depend on the Lord, you are content as you pursue His goals for your life.

Read Psalm 128:1–2; Proverbs 3:5–6; 22:17–19; Philippians 4:11–13; 2 Corinthians 3:5; 1 Timothy 6:6–16.

Questions:

How would you reconcile Paul's statements "I have learned to be content," and "I can do all things through Christ?"

_____

_____

_____

_____

_____

In looking back at your walk with the Lord thus far, how can you see that you have grown in this area?

_____

_____

_____

_____

_____

_____

What has been the result of increased trust in God and acceptance of His will in your life?

_____

_____

_____

_____

_____

Word Wealth—*Content*

Content: Greek *autarkes* (ow-tar'-kace); Strong's #842: to experience sufficiency, to possess enough, to be satisfied, to experience no want or lack. To be content in the Lord is to recognize that He is *Jehovah Jireh* (Genesis 22:14—The

Lord our Provider). We can be content knowing His very name assures that He will take it upon Himself to supply all our needs as He determines. Realizing God's love and accepting God's rule will result in absolute contentment.

 Kingdom Extra—*Worry and Discontent*

Two powerful weapons deployed by satan against God's people are worry and discontent. Both will result in a life filled with anxiety and chaos. And unfortunately, they seem to come as a package deal. Where you find discontentment, you will discover worry; where there is worry, contentment is not to be found.

Worry paralyzes active faith in your life. When you worry, you assume responsibility for things you were never intended to handle. Jesus repeatedly taught: "Do not worry" (the Greek word *merimne* meaning "to divide the mind"), even about the basic essentials of life. Worry changes nothing but divides your mind between useful and harmful thinking. It draws your focus away from God and His faithfulness to the concerns about the things of life. Worry is a choking, harmful emotion that saps your energy and elevates human strength and ingenuity above God's rule, strength and plan.

Discontent rejects what exists for the lure of an imagined better way. When we perceive that a circumstance does not meet our idea of perfection, we look for something better. This way of thinking leads us on an endless chase because at the end of every rainbow, we will only find something different lacking. Perfection will never be found outside the only One who is perfect. A tireless quest for change won't satisfy us; change in and of itself will never supply contentment. Only Jesus can satisfy us and only in Him can we rest contentedly.

We are helpless and lost without God, who keeps all His promises. Our best state of life is contentment, a life free of worry and restlessness. Contentment will enable us to freely obey God and resist temptations to follow the ways of the world to provide our own perceived needs. Contentment recognizes our need for God and His ability and willingness to rule our lives in love.

Read Psalm 23:1–6; 112:7–8; Proverbs 30:5; Matthew 6:25–34; 6:31; Luke 10:40–42.

Questions:

Locate Scriptures instructing us not to worry.

✎ _____

_____

_____

_____

_____

What must exist in our lives in order for us to carry out the scriptural mandate against worry?

✎ _____

_____

_____

What are areas of discontent in your life?

✎ _____

_____

_____

How does this negatively affect your relationship with the Lord?

✎ _____

_____

_____

_____

Probing the Depths—*He is God and We are Not*

The Psalms reveal much of God's nature. The following table contains statements made in the Psalms about God. Look up the references as you read through.

THE LORD IS . . .	ACCORDING TO PSALMS
Creator of the world	• The heavens, the moon, and the stars are the "work of His fingers" (8:3) • "He commanded and they were created" (148:5). • He "laid the foundations of the earth" (104:5). • He gives all creatures life (104:27–30).[1]
All-Powerful	• He laughs when human rulers conspire together against Him (2:4). • "The voice of the LORD shakes the wilderness" (29:8). • His power causes even His enemies to submit to Him (66:3).
All-Wise	• In His wisdom He created the world (104:24). • He is the starting point for wisdom (111:10). • He knows everything we do and say (139:2–4).[2]
Eternal	• "From everlasting to everlasting, You are God" (90:2). • "You are from everlasting" (93:2). • "You are the same, and Your years will have no end" 102:27).
Holy	• "God sits on His holy throne" (47:8). • "He is holy" (99:3, 5, 9). • "Holy and awesome is His name" (111:9).

---

[1] Thomas Nelson, Inc., *Word in Life Study Bible* [*computer file*], electronic ed., Logos Library System, (Nashville: Thomas Nelson) 1997, © 1996.
[2] Thomas Nelson, Inc., *Word in Life Study Bible* [*computer file*], electronic ed., Logos Library System, (Nashville: Thomas Nelson) 1997, © 1996.

THE LORD IS . . .	ACCORDING TO PSALMS
Good	• "Good and upright is the LORD" (25:8). • "The LORD is good" (100:5). • "The LORD is righteous in all His ways" (145:17).
Merciful and Forgiving	• "All the paths of the LORD are mercy and truth" (25:10). • "His mercy endures forever" (136:1–26). • He forgives all our iniquities (103:3).
Faithful	• "Those who know Your name will put their trust in You; for • You, LORD, have not forsaken those who seek You" (9:10). • "He who keeps you will not slumber" (121:3).
Personally and intimately involved with His creatures	• He fashions the hearts of people individually (33:15). • "He causes the grass to grow for the cattle, and vegetation for the service of man" (104:14). • "You formed my inward parts" (139:13).
True and straightforward	• "The judgments of the LORD are true and righteous altogether" (19:9). • He is the "LORD God of truth" (31:5). • All His commandments are truth (119:151).
Just	• "God is a just judge" (7:11). • "He loves righteousness and justice" (33:5). • He "executes justice for the oppressed" (146:7).

Read Psalm 18:31; Proverbs 3:19–20; 8:21–35.

Questions:

Do your actions reflect the knowledge that you are not God?

✎ _____

_____

_____

What things do you tend to allow to rule in your life?

✎ _____

_____

_____

 Kingdom Life—*We Are Accountable*

There is no one like the Lord, the Almighty One, whose glory fills the universe. Although the kingdom is God's, God gives resources that are man's to administrate. God is the fountainhead of all life and power; man is the appointed heir for its management. While the created universe and the glory of the heavens are God's and God's alone, He has delegated the stewardship of Earth's affairs to mankind. Noble views of God's sovereignty must be balanced with a complementary view of man's duties and redeemed capacities. Neglect of this balance, while seeming to extol God's greatness, can produce apathy or irresponsible attitudes. For example, God does not predestine mismanaged resources, families, politics, and so on, any more than He does human sinning. Man is responsible and accountable for Earth's problems and—reinstated under God—is intended to become the agent for their solution. However, he can only become such by drawing on God's sovereign wisdom, power, and resource, that is, on God's "kingdom." Just as man's sin and fall have damaged the potential partnership between the Creator and His appointed heir to this planet, redemption has set the recovery in motion. Renewed under God, the redeemed may, in fact, partner with God and thereby decisively assist in the reestablishment of God's rule over circumstances and situations on Earth. But this only operates under the divine order within redemption's plan under divine grace and through man's receiving divine power by God's Spirit.

Read Psalm 8:6 and 115:16.

Questions:

In what ways do you experience your reinstated dominion in God?

✎ _____

_____

_____

_____

What might you change in your life to discover this partnership to a greater degree?

✎ _____

_____

_____

_____

_____

_____

Invite God's Rule

It is foolish to think man could add to or diminish the power or glory of God's kingdom rule. However, it is equally unwise to overlook the responsible place the redeemed have been given. We are to *welcome* the kingdom and administer situations on earth by inviting the overarching might of God's Spirit to move into difficult or impossible circumstances and transform them. This is done by praise: "In everything [not "for" everything] give thanks [fill the situation with praise], for this is God's will for you" (1 Thessalonians 5:17). Thus we welcome the overruling power of God's presence into any situation we face. Pray, "Your kingdom come, Your will be done—here." Then, set up a place for God's throne to enter by filling your life's settings with praise. As Gideon's trumpeters (Judges 7:17–22) and Jehoshaphat's choir (2 Chronicles 20:20–22) confounded their enemies and paved the way for the victory the Lord said He would give, so praise brings the same entry of the King's kingdom today.

Read Psalm 93:2; 1 Thessalonians 5:17.

Questions:

What Scriptures can you discover that give further insight into the power of praise?

Is a heart of praise alive and well within you?

How do you see this affecting your walk with the Lord?

Kingdom Life—*Establish God's Throne*

Few principles are more essential to our understanding of the Kingdom than this one: the *presence* of God's kingdom power is directly related to the practice of God's *praise*. We are told in Psalm 22:3 that God is "enthroned in the praises of Israel." The verb "enthroned" indicates that wherever God's people exalt His name, He is ready to manifest His kingdom's power in the way most appropriate to the situation, as His rule is invited to invade our setting.

It is this fact that properly leads many to conclude that in a very real way, praise prepares a *specific* and *present* place for God among His people. Some have chosen the term "establish His throne" to describe this "enthroning" of God in our midst by our worshipping and praising welcome. God awaits the prayerful and praise-filled worship of His people as an entry point for His kingdom to "come"—to enter, that *His* "will be done" in human circumstances. We do not manipulate God, but align ourselves with the great kingdom truth: *His* is the power, ours is the privilege (and responsibility) to welcome Him into our world—our private, present world or the circumstances of our society.

Read Psalm 93:2; 100; Luke 11:2–4.

Record Your Thoughts

Reread Psalm 128.

Questions:

In what way does the Psalmist express his praise to God?

_____

_____

_____

_____

_____

What does it mean to live a life of praise?

_____

_____

_____

_____

What will be God's response to a heart of praise?

_____

_____

_____

_____

_____

The Way of the Wise

Proverbs 2—4: Conclusion

Kingdom Key—*Fear God*

Proverbs 9:10 The fear of the Lord is the beginning of wisdom, and the knowledge of the Holy One is understanding.

Wisdom is an eternal cycle, ever revolving around the source of all wisdom. It is, at once, the driving force that compels us to seek and know our God, and the result of having attained our desire. The greatest reward that comes from wisdom is the fear and knowledge of God, just as, the fear and knowledge of God will birth wisdom within us. Wisdom, then, is vitally connected with knowing God and having a proper relationship with Him.

Read Psalms 51:6; Proverbs 2:6; James 1:4; Colossians 2:1–10.

Question:

What does it mean to "fear" God?

Word Wealth—*Fear*

Fear: Hebrew *yirah* (yir-aw); Strong's #3374: to be fearfully reverent. At its core *yarah* is to revere or stand in awe of the power and position of another. *Yarah* is to render proper respect and submission to God. The root of *yarah* is *yare* which can also connote an awesome presence or awe-inspiring effect.

A Crown for Today

Read Proverbs 4:9.

Wisdom will deliver to us a "crown of glory." The word "crown" in Proverbs 4:9 is used as a symbol of victory, reward, and honor. The word in Hebrew, *atarahŌ*, refers to a headpiece of great beauty that signifies command or superiority, as in a king or ruler.

Look up the following passages and summarize what each says about the *spiritual* meanings of "crown."

Isaiah 28:5

Revelation 19:12

Proverbs 12:4

Proverbs 17:6

Proverbs 20:29

Kingdom Life—*Seek Wisdom*

The Scripture tells us God will bless us exceedingly if we seek wisdom. The Lord Jesus told us something similar in Matthew 6:33, that if we seek the rule of God over our lives and His righteousness, His ways to do rightly, all the things of this life and the next that we need He will provide.

The spirit of Wisdom will lead us to identify anything in our lives that needs to be changed in order for us to bring our lives into line with the will of God. Yielding to His rule over us will pave the way for wisdom's rewards. Rejecting God's rule will rob us of the blessings of His kingdom.

Read Proverbs 3:5–12; 2:10–22; 4:10–19, 22; 4:7–13, 22.

Questions:

What benefits do we receive when we seek to operate in God's wisdom?

_____

_____

_____

_____

Do you experience these in your own life?

_____

_____

_____

The Greatest Wisdom Focuses on God

We have seen all the blessings that flow from a life of wisdom. The greatest of those blessings is the knowledge of God. The greatest of all wisdom's children is spiritual wisdom, the wisdom which focuses on God Himself.

Read Proverbs 3:1–6.

Questions:

Define wisdom in your own words.

✎ _____

_____

_____

_____

_____

Do you experience the earthly benefits of wisdom in your own life?

✎ _____

_____

_____

Compare your life to Proverbs 3:5–6. What do you see lacking?

✎ _____

_____

_____

_____

Probing the Depths—*Review*

The spirit of wisdom is none other than the Spirit of God. Wisdom possesses all the attributes of God Himself. As you review the themes and Kingdom Keys of this in-depth look at wisdom, determine which part of God's nature is revealed by each. What does each require of you?

1. **The Way of Blessing—Avoid Evil**

✎ _____

_____

_____

_____

2. The Way of Righteousness—Know the Lord

_____

_____

_____

_____

_____

3. The Way of Character—Give Generously

_____

_____

_____

_____

_____

4. The Way of Abundance—Persevere

_____

_____

_____

_____

5. The Way of Humility—Recognize God's Preeminence

_____

_____

_____

_____

6. The Way of Freedom—Listen and Obey

_____

_____

_____

_____

_____

7. The Way of Favor—Be Diligent

_____
_____
_____
_____
_____

8. The Way of Confidence—Rely on God

_____
_____
_____
_____
_____

9. The Way of Courage—Find Strength in the Lord

_____
_____
_____
_____

10. The Way of Worth—Abide in God

_____
_____
_____
_____

11. The Way of Contentment—Follow Faithfully

_____
_____
_____
_____
_____

12. The Way of the Wise—Fear the Lord

_____

_____

_____

_____

Christians are called by God to live righteous, holy lives of respon-sible, wise behavior. Wisdom is a pathway of right choices, acknowl-edging our own inability and God's supreme authority. We are told in James 1:5, "If any of you lacks wisdom, let him ask of God, who gives to all liberally and without reproach, and it will be given to him." So ask and receive. Wisdom allows us to trust God with all the situations of life and to respond positively to His correction. Wisdom will lead us to walk in love, considering others above ourselves. Through wis-dom we will be greatly blessed and be able to bless others as well.

Read Psalm 111:10; Proverbs 2:6–10; 4:5–7; 11:12; 15:33.

Question:

How does love relate to the way of wisdom?

_____

_____

_____

_____

Word Wealth—*Wisdom*

Wisdom: Greek *sophia* (sof-ee'-ah); Strong's #4678: Prudence, skill, compre-hensive insight, Christian enlightenment, a right application of knowledge, insight into the true nature of things.

Record Your Thoughts

Look up all the references you can find to the "fear of the Lord."

✎_____

_____

_____

_____

Why do you believe this is the beginning and heart of wisdom?

✎_____

_____

_____

_____

Review the Session Themes and Kingdom Keys. How might love enable you to walk in the ways they represent?

✎_____

_____

_____

_____

Read James 1:5: If any of you lacks wisdom, let him ask of God, who gives to all liberally and without reproach, and it will be given to him.

Printed in the USA
CPSIA information can be obtained
at www.ICGtesting.com
LVHW011151281223
767070LV00005B/13